RACEPLANE TECH SERIES

VOLUME 2

W9-DCI-050

ROUND-ENGINE RACERS

BEARCATS & CORSAIRS

NICHOLAS A. VERONICO AND A. KEVIN GRANTHAM

specialtypress
PUBLISHERS AND WHOLESALERS

Published by
Specialty Press Publishers and Wholesalers
39966 Grand Avenue
North Branch, MN 55056
United States of America
(800) 895-4585 or (651) 277-1400
http://www.specialtypress.com

Distributed in the UK and Europe by
Midland Publishing
4 Watling Drive
Hinckley LE10 3EY, England
Tel: 01455 233 747 Fax: 01455 233 737
http://www.midlandcountiessuperstore.com

ISBN 1-58007-035-3

Printed in China

Title Page: *During the third lap Number 74's intake valves opened while the Triptane was still burning. The resulting backfire dislodged the scoop. Here Becker is taxiing his racer back to the pit after making an emergency landing.* (Emil Strasser via Gerry Liang)

Front Cover: *The round engine racer with the most Unlimited Class wins is Lyle Shelton's Rare Bear, turning over for the start of the 1994 Unlimited Gold Race. Both Shelton and John Penney have won flying the racer.* (Nicholas A. Veronico)

Back Cover (Left Top): *For the 1992 Unlimited Gold Race, Kevin Eldridge flew the R-4360-powered Corsair to a sixth place finish at an average speed of 420.800 mph. Stiletto, the highly modified Merlin-powered Mustang that has had its belly scoop removed and the radiators installed in the wing roots, was flown by Matt Jackson to a fourth place finish (426.563 mph). Gary Levitz, in the P-51D Miss Ashley, finished seventh (378.344 mph).* (Nicholas A. Veronico)

Back Cover (Right Top): *Lyle Shelton had flown one series at Reno and was preparing for the 1970 racing season at Compton Airport in Southern California when this photo was shot in August. Tony Bernard stands near the aircraft's starboard main gear, while Cliff Putnam, left on wing, and Lyle Shelton, right, button the aircraft up prior to an engine run.* (Chris McMillin)

Back Cover (Right Lower): *In the complex inner workings of the Wright R-3350, exploding fuel is converted into horsepower to drive the crankshaft, connecting rods, rear cam, vibration balancer, and drive.* (National Archives)

TABLE OF CONTENTS

BEARCATS & CORSAIRS

PREFACE

A WORD FROM THE AUTHORS

This book is dedicated to Armand H. Veronico and Oliver Aldrich, who introduced air racing to the authors.

The debate between which type of aircraft is faster or stronger—those powered by round motors or in-line engines—is never ending. Can a Merlin engine hold together at high manifold pressures and rpms for a sustained period, or will the dependability of an R-3350 or R-4360 prevail? And don't forget about that wild card lurking on the racecourse—the Rolls-Royce Griffon-powered Mustang. The fact of the matter is that round-engine racers have taxied into the winner's circle 17 times out of the 36 Unlimited races run at Reno.

Throughout the history of air racing, three eras have been defined: the Golden Age (1919–1939), the postwar era (1946–1949), and "modern air racing" (1964 to present). Within modern air racing, it can be further separated into three eras: the Greenamyer years (1965–1970), when *Conquest I* dominated the pylon racing circuit; the modified Mustang years (1972–1982), when racers such as the *Roto-Finish Special*, *Red Baron*, *Sumthin' Else*, *Jeannie*, and *Dago Red* ruled the skies; and the "supermodified" years (1983 to present), when such highly modified craft as *Dreadnought*, the *Pond Racer*, *Rare Bear*, *Stiletto*, *Strega*, the *Super Corsair*, *Tsunami*, and *Voodoo* battled one another for the Unlimited Gold trophy. Three racers have owned the supermodified years: Lyle Shelton

and John Penney in *Rare Bear* (Reno Unlimited Gold victories in 1988–1991 and 1994), Bill "Tiger" Destefani in *Strega* (Reno: 1987, 1992, 1993, 1995–1997), and Bruce Lockwood and Skip Holm in *Dago Red* (Reno: 1998–2000). Sadly, due to the terrorist attacks on September 11, 2001, the Federal Aviation Administration canceled the National Championship Air Races at Reno, thus no champion was crowned that year.

The list of modern era race pilots who have won Reno's Unlimited Gold (known as the Unlimited Championship Race from 1964 through 1979, with the Unlimited Bronze, Silver and Gold Races beginning in 1980) while flying a Bearcat or Corsair contains only seven names: Mira Slovak (in Bill Stead's Bearcat), Darryl Greenamyer (in *Conquest I*), Lyle Shelton (in *Rare Bear*), Neil Anderson (*Dreadnought*), Steve Hinton (*Super Corsair*), the late Rick Brickert (*Dreadnought*), and John Penney (*Rare Bear*). It is the racing prowess of these champions and their outstanding competition that are chronicled on the following pages.

The authors owe a debt of gratitude to those in the air racing community for their time, knowledge, and support for the RaceplaneTech Series. They include: Gene Akers, Richard Allnutt, Chuck Aro, Shawn Aro, James R. Axtell, Brian Baker,

Pete Behenna, Ray and Caroline Bingham, Peter M. Bowers, John Brooks, Roger Cain, Logan Coombs, Ed Davies, John Davis, Jim Dunn, Phil Edwards, Kevin Eldridge, Wayne Gomes, Jackie Grantham, Karen B. Haack, Todd Hackbarth, Dan Hagedorn, Al Hansen, Ervan Hare, Jim Hawkins, Steve Hinton, Earl Holmquist, Richard Johnson (MAPS Air Museum), Norm Jukes, Aaron King, John Kirk, Tom Kraft, Tillie and William T. Larkins, Jim Larsen, Gerry Liang, Chris McMillin, Brian Nicholas, Neal Nurmi, Dan O'Hara, Betty Olinger, Dave Ostrowski, Bob Pauley, Dick Phillips, Taigh Ramey, Ron Reynolds, Harrison Rued, Bernie Schulte, David Schwartz, Randy Scoville, John Slack, Lyle Shelton, Larry Smigla, Kevin Smith, Charles E. Stewart and Chuck Stewart, Ron Strong, Scott Thompson, Paul Varga, Armand Veronico, Betty Veronico, Tony Veronico, and Tim Weinschenker. Brett Wilson of Wilson Illustration and Design (   ) provided the artwork for volumes one and two of the *RaceplaneTech Series*.

Nicholas A. Veronico
San Carlos, California

A. Kevin Grantham
Frederick, Maryland

Go Fast !

Production models of both the Vought F4U Corsair and the Grumman F8F Bearcat were powered by the 18-cylinder Pratt & Whitney R-2800 Double Wasp air-cooled radial engine. At the time of its introduction, the R-2800 was one of the most powerful engines on the planet, but with the need for bigger and faster airplanes, larger engines emerged. These bigger engines, such the Wright R-3350 and the massive Pratt & Whitney R-4360, were originally conceived for larger bombers and transport airplanes. However, in 1943 Pratt & Whitney grafted an R-4360 onto a stock F4U-1 (F4U-1WM, Bureau number 02460) and created what many call the "Super Corsair." Goodyear eventually converted and constructed a total of 17 R-4360-powered Corsairs before the war ended. What has happened in air racing since the end of World War II mirrors in some ways what Vought, Goodyear, and Pratt & Whitney did at a time when faster interceptors were needed to thwart enemy attackers.

During the past 55 years, racing Bearcats and Corsairs have appeared in pylon and cross-country events at various venues around the United States. Many had different configurations, ranging from stock to super-modified, but all were powered by one of three radial engine types; namely the Pratt & Whitney R-2800, the Wright Aeronautical R-3350, or the Pratt & Whitney R-4360.

PRATT & WHITNEY R-2800 DOUBLE WASP

Pratt & Whitney's R-2800 Double Wasp was the first successful 18-cylinder radial engine built in the United States. Development of the R-2800 began in 1937 with the intent of building an engine that could produce 1,800 horsepower. The resulting powerplant was capable of delivering approximately 100 horsepower per cylinder, and later versions were rated with a total power output as high as 2,000 horsepower.

Handling unwanted heat is the master trade-off to achieving high power ratings in an engine. To deal with this problem, Pratt & Whitney engineers cleverly machined ultra-thin, fine-pitched cooling fins deep into the cylinder head forging to help cool each cylinder. This was a departure from using only cast cooling fins. The machining process was both time-consuming and expensive, but the results proved to be very effective. Pratt & Whitney also invested a great deal of time in researching air baffling to better steer

Pratt & Whitney set out to produce an engine that had the same profile as a standard two-row radial engine but with twice the power. It developed the R-2800, which weighed 2,360 pounds and was capable of producing 2,000 horsepower while turning at 2,700 rpm with 54 inches on manifold pressure—nearly one horsepower per pound. The R-2800's construction includes a three-piece forged aluminum alloy crankcase. Its cylinders have steel barrels and shrunk-on forged aluminum cooling muffs and heads. Each cylinder has one sodium-cooled inlet and exhaust valve. (National Archives)

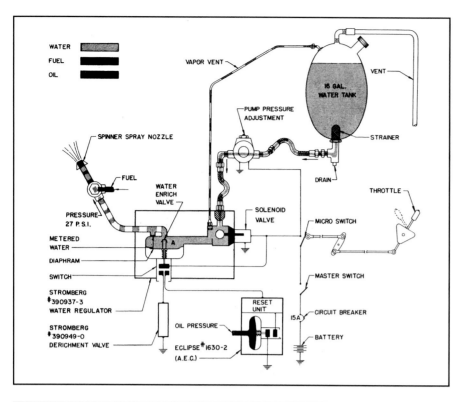

WATER
FUEL
OIL

VAPOR VENT

16 GAL. WATER TANK

VENT

PUMP PRESSURE ADJUSTMENT

STRAINER

SPINNER SPRAY NOZZLE

FUEL

DRAIN

THROTTLE

WATER ENRICH VALVE

SOLENOID VALVE

MICRO SWITCH

PRESSURE 27 P.S.I.

METERED WATER

DIAPHRAM

SWITCH

STROMBERG #390937-3 WATER REGULATOR

STROMBERG #390949-0 DERICHMENT VALVE

MASTER SWITCH

RESET UNIT

OIL PRESSURE

ECLIPSE #1630-2 (A.E.C.)

CIRCUIT BREAKER

15A

BATTERY

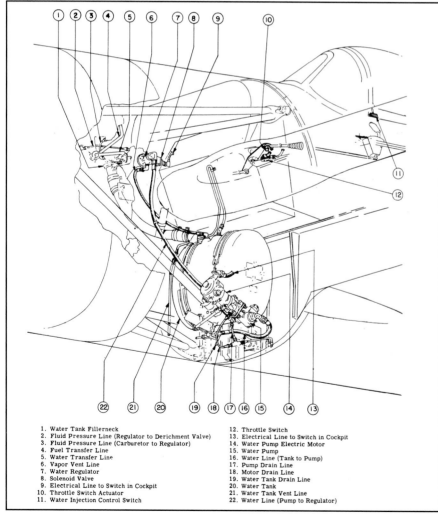

1. Water Tank Fillerneck
2. Fluid Pressure Line (Regulator to Derichment Valve)
3. Fluid Pressure Line (Carburetor to Regulator)
4. Fuel Transfer Line
5. Water Transfer Line
6. Vapor Vent Line
7. Water Regulator
8. Solenoid Valve
9. Electrical Line to Switch in Cockpit
10. Throttle Switch Actuator
11. Water Injection Control Switch
12. Throttle Switch
13. Electrical Line to Switch in Cockpit
14. Water Pump Electric Motor
15. Water Pump
16. Water Line (Tank to Pump)
17. Pump Drain Line
18. Motor Drain Line
19. Water Tank Drain Line
20. Water Tank
21. Water Tank Vent Line
22. Water Line (Pump to Regulator)

Schematic of the water injection system and its installation in the F8F-2. The water tank was installed in the lower area of the engine accessory section, ahead of the firewall. Water injection gave production Bearcats the ability to climb at 4,800 feet per minute and reach a top speed of 424 mph. (National Archives)

cooling air where it was most needed. In the end, Pratt & Whitney's R-2800 design efforts produced an engine that many feel is the finest piston radial engine ever built.

Production of the R-2800 began in 1940, followed by the engine's first application in the Martin B-26 in December of the same year. Production of the Double Wasp was stepped up after the attack on Pearl Harbor. Almost every aircraft manufacturer in the country had a design that called for the R-2800. Grumman coupled it with its F6F Hellcat, F8F Bearcat, and twin engine F7F Tigercat design, while Republic chose the R-2800 for its new P-47 Thunderbolt. Douglas and Northup also selected the engine to power the A-26 Invader and the P-61 Black Widow.

PRATT & WHITNEY'S DESCRIPTION OF THE R-2800 *

"The Double Wasp engine itself consists of a three-piece aluminum crankcase assembled with bolts into a single rugged unit. Space-saving, lead silver main bearings permit the use of sufficient metal in the crankcase to provide rigid support of the main bearings. The magnesium propeller reduction gear housing contains the deep, ball-grooved, ball thrust bearings, six torque meter pistons and a helically splined, axially floating ring gear. The propeller

---

* Reprinted with permission.

RACEPLANE TECH SERIES

shaft and pinion cage are made from a single steel forging.

"The Double Wasp's cylinders feature three principal components—a forged steel barrel and mounting flange, a deep-finned, forged aluminum cooling sleeve or muff, and a forged duraluminum cylinder head, with deep, machine-cut cooling fins. The muff is shrunk on the forged steel cylinder barrel and the cylinder head is both screwed and shrunk on the barrel to produce the strongest and most trouble-free cylinder unit ever produced.

"In the rear main crankcase are the double track cam for the rear cylinders, the cam and cam reduction gears, and the tappets and the secondary counterbalance with its drive gear. The counterbalance is driven through an intermediate gear. At the hub of the supercharger impeller and rotating at impeller shaft speed is the perforated spinner fuel injection ring, which centrifugally sprays a curtain of finely divided fuel, or fuel and water, across the intake air stream at the supercharger throat.

"Mounted on the rear face of the accessory case are the main oil pressure and scavenge pumps, and drives and mounting pads for starter, generator, power takeoff, and fuel pump. On the sides of the case are drives and mounting pads for vacuum or hydraulic pumps and tachometer generators. The downdraft, pressure injection carburetor, and water regulator are mounted on the upper section of the accessory case."

WRIGHT R-3350 CYCLONE

The Wright Aeronautical Corporation's R-3350 Cyclone was one of the most powerful and most troublesome radial aircraft engines produced during World War II. The initial design of the R-3350 was started in 1936 in response to U.S. government contracts for aircraft being developed by Consolidated, Douglas, and Martin. Wright engineers based the new engine scheme on the company's R-2600 design, and both powerplants shared the same bore (6.125 inches) and stroke (6.3125 inches) in addition to many similar components. However, unlike the successful R-2600, Wright experienced many problems with its R-3350 design.

The distribution of fuel vapor to the engine's 18 cylinders was not uniform. This resulted in random cylinders getting more fuel than others, making for an uneven running engine. Early R-3350s also had a bad tendency to backfire. The R-3350 carried large amounts of fuel mixture through the induction system between the carburetors and the cylinders, and this presented a potential fire hazard when the engine backfired. Both the fuel distribution and the backfiring problems were eventually solved, when Wright Aeronautical introduced the direct fuel injection R-3350-57 variant toward the end of the World War II. This scheme allowed the fuel to be injected directly into the combustion chamber, while the induction passages were only used for intro-

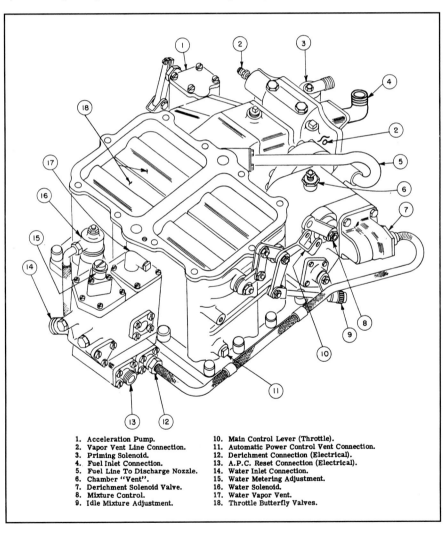

1. Acceleration Pump.
2. Vapor Vent Line Connection.
3. Priming Solenoid.
4. Fuel Inlet Connection.
5. Fuel Line To Discharge Nozzle.
6. Chamber "Vent".
7. Derichment Solenoid Valve.
8. Mixture Control.
9. Idle Mixture Adjustment.
10. Main Control Lever (Throttle).
11. Automatic Power Control Vent Connection.
12. Derichment Connection (Electrical).
13. A.P.C. Reset Connection (Electrical).
14. Water Inlet Connection.
15. Water Metering Adjustment.
16. Water Solenoid.
17. Water Vapor Vent.
18. Throttle Butterfly Valves.

Carburetor installation as fitted to the 2,100-horsepower R-2800-34W on the F8F-2 Bearcat. (National Archives)

Cutaway of the turbocompound R-3350, which displaced 3,347 cubic inches. Turbocompound R-3350s gave reliable service to the airlines for many years. The R-3350 in Rare Bear *uses the reduction gear mechanism from a Lockheed 1649 Constellation.* (National Archives)

ducing air to the cylinder. Cooling the big engine was also one of the most serious problems that faced Wright engineers during the early stages of the R-3350's development.

Boeing's B-29 Superfortress was designed around the R-3350 powerplant, and airflow through the B-29's low-drag engine cowls was critical. The cylinder heads on the R-3350 were made of cast aluminum. The cylinder's finning surface, from an initial design standpoint, appeared sufficient to remove the desired heat, but in reality did not keep the B-29 engine from overheating. This was particularly true of the cylinders in the back row of the R-3350, and in some cases the cylinders would reach temperatures high enough to ignite the magnesium casting around the supercharger. A fire of this type could not be extinguished in the air and often resulted in the loss of the aircraft. Wright engineers researched the problem and eventually produced a solution in the form of improved cast cylinder heads, as well as using new cylinder heads machined from a solid block of aluminum.

Wright began work on the R-3350 design in 1935. The engine is most famous for powering the B-29 and later the Lockheed Constellation and Douglas DC-7. During the war, the engine was cantankerous; it ran rough, overheated, and was prone to catching fire. Most of the bugs were worked out of the design when fuel injection was introduced near the end of the war. The R-3350 went on to be an extremely reliable engine for airline service, and powered Douglas's Skyraider family of ground attack fighters. R-3350-powered Constellations flew the line until the type was retired in favor of jet-powered aircraft in the mid-1960s. (National Archives)

Pratt & Whitney's R-4360 Wasp Major engine was the largest piston engine ever to enter production. Stock engines featured a single-stage, variable speed supercharger. In addition to the F2G Corsair series, the engine powered Boeing's civil and military versions of the Stratocruiser, and Douglas's C-74 and C-124 Globemasters. The men working on the R-4360 lend scale to the R-4360's size. (National Archives)

Wright Aeronautical continued to develop the R-3350 after World War II, and what began as a very troublesome project grew up to be a very reliable product that was widely used by the aircraft industry. In 1950, Wright Aeronautical introduced the Turbo-Compound R-3350. The exhaust gases of this engine were used to drive three turbines. Each turbine fed six cylinders and this configuration boosted the engine's power by approximately 600 horsepower without burning any extra fuel. The Turbo-Compound R-3350 found great success in various military and civilian designs through the 1950s.

PRATT & WHITNEY R-4360 WASP MAJOR

In 1939, Luke Hobb, vice president of Pratt & Whitney, set out to design an engine that would have the same frontal profile as the R-2800, but with double the power rating. The major problem with such a design, as it was with both the R-2800 and the Wright R-3350, was

with cooling. In 1939, no engine manufacturer in the United States had looked into the problems of removing heat from an engine with more than two rows of cylinders. Hobbs got around the problem by offsetting each successive row of seven cylinders in a spiral arrangement around the one-piece steel forged crankshaft, allowing cooling air to be directly ducted to each section of the motor.

The piston displacement of this new 28-cylinder design measured 4,360 cubic inches with a bore of 5.75 inches and stroke of 6 inches. All of the cylinders were interchangeable and had steel barrels with shrunk-on forged aluminum muffs and forged aluminum alloy heads. The rod assembly for each cylinder row accounted for one master rod with lead-silver bearings, and six linked rods. The power section crankcase of the R-4360 consisted of five sections machined from aluminum forgings. The other crankcase sections were made of magnesium castings. The front part of the power section supported seven magnetos and housed

the planetary spur reduction gear (ratio 0.381:1 or 0.425:1), torquemeter, and accouterments for a Hydromatic propeller. The aft power section included mounting arrangements for a gear-driven supercharger and a Stromberg PR100B3 four-barrel, downdraft injection, pressure-type carburetor.

Pratt & Whitney was awarded a government contract to pursue the development of the R-4360 in late 1940, and the engine's first run occurred in April of the following year. In May 1942, a modified Consolidated Vultee Model 85 Vengeance was the first aircraft to fly using the Wasp Major as its powerplant. It took Pratt & Whitney approximately two years and 20,000 man-hours of development time to get the R-4360 into production. Satisfied with the performance of the R-4360-powered F4U-1WM, the Navy's Bureau of Aeronautics issued Contract Number 2971 to Goodyear for 418 R-4360-powered Corsairs (designated F2G). The F2G would not be ready in time to influence the outcome of World War II,

Below: *In the complex inner workings of the Wright R-3350, exploding fuel is converted into horsepower to drive the crankshaft, connecting rods, rear cam, vibration balancer, and drive.* (National Archives)

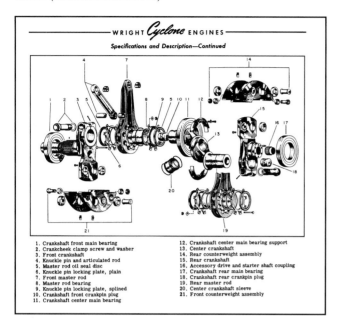

1. Crankshaft front main bearing
2. Crankcheek clamp screw and washer
3. Front crankshaft
4. Knuckle pin and articulated rod
5. Master rod oil seal disc
6. Knuckle pin locking plate, plain
7. Front master rod
8. Master rod bearing
9. Knuckle pin locking plate, splined
10. Crankshaft front crankpin plug
11. Crankshaft center main bearing
12. Crankshaft center main bearing support
13. Center crankshaft
14. Rear counterweight assembly
15. Rear crankshaft
16. Accessory drive and starter shaft coupling
17. Crankshaft rear main bearing
18. Crankshaft rear crankpin plug
19. Rear master rod
20. Center crankshaft sleeve
21. Front counterweight assembly

1. Piston pin and plug
2. Cylinder barrel to crankcase main section oil seal ring
3. Front cylinder
4. Push rod housing connection
5. Cylinder head fin brace spring
6. Push rod housing connection upper nut locking screw
7. Rocker lubricating tube connector
8. Rocker lubricating tube
9. Rocker arm shaft bushings
10. Valve spring outer lower washer
11. Exhaust valve seat
12. Exhaust valve guide
13. Intake valve seat
14. Cylinder head air deflector
15. Rocker box cover
16. Intake valve guide
17. Intake valve spring inner lower washer
18. Fuel injection nozzle insert
19. Spark plug insert
20. Thermocouple adapter
21. Front exhaust pipe connection
22. Front exhaust pipe
23. Front exhaust pipe to collector ring clamp
24. Intake pipe connection
25. Piston and rings

Above Right: *Cylinder assembly of an R-3350 featured a 6.125-inch bore and 6.3125-inch stroke. The cooling fins of the early war, cast aluminum cylinder heads did not have enough area to dissipate sufficient heat. Later engines featured improved cast cylinder heads, and eventually units machined from solid aluminum blocks.* (National Archives)

but it played a significant role in proving out Luke Hobb's original design concept for a high-powered, multiple-row radial engine. After World War II, the Pratt & Whitney R-4360 continued its success and remained in production until 1955.

Each engine type has had its turn in the Unlimited class winner's circle. As racers became more sophisticated, the R-2800 was outclassed. The round-engine racing champions of the new millennium will continue to consistently turn the pylons in the 450-plus-mph range, as demonstrated by the R-4360's brute horsepower or reach the 500 mph range with heavily modified versions of the R-3350, as demonstrated by *Rare Bear*. No matter the engine choice, in-line or radial, unlimited air racing will remain the fastest motorsport, and one of the best spectator sports in the world.

Vought transferred BuNo 02460 to Pratt & Whitney for installation trials of the XR-4360 in March 1943. Compare the Corsair at left, equipped with the Wasp Major, to the stock F4U-1 at right. The intake scoop for the R-4360's downdraft carburetor seems too short and out of place. When R-4360-powered F2Gs raced at Cleveland, the carburetor intake scoop was extended to the edge of the cowling. (Vought via National Archives)

RACEPLANE**TECH**
S E R I E S

RACING 2CORSAIRS

One of the most successful naval fighters of World War II was the Vought-designed F4U Corsair. Built by Vought, Goodyear, and Brewster, 12,582 were constructed between 1940 and 1952. During the aircraft's operational career, the Corsair was flown by the U.S. Navy and Marine Corps, the British Fleet Air Arm, French Aeronavale, Honduran Air Force (Fuerza Aerea Hondurena), El Salvadorean Air Force (Fuerza Aerea Salvadorena), and Royal New Zealand Air Force. The Corsair featured an inverted gull-wing and a 2,000-horsepower Pratt & Whitney R-2800 radial engine.

During the war, the U.S. Navy determined that the fleet needed a point defense fighter capable of climbing to altitude and intercepting enemy fighters moments after launch. To meet this requirement, the Navy instructed Vought Aircraft to transfer F4U-1 BuNo 02460 to Pratt & Whitney on March 25, 1943. The engine manufacturer mated a prototype 3,000-horsepower, 28-cylinder, air-cooled XR-4360 radial engine to the Corsair as a proof of concept to show that the most powerful piston engine to enter production could power the Corsair. Bureau Number 02460 was redesignated the sole F4U-1WM for "Wasp Major." Subsequently, on February 7, 1944, the U.S. Navy's Bureau of Aeronautics Engineering Division contracted with Goodyear Aircraft, Akron, Ohio, to develop the Wasp Major-powered variant of the Corsair that would be designated F2G.

The production F2G was built in two different models: the F2G-1, a land-based, nonfolding wing interceptor intended for the U.S. Marine Corps; and the F2G-2, a carrier-based fighter with increased fuel capacity and armament. Both models were powered by the R-4360 radial engine. Goodyear had to make several design changes to the basic FG-1 airframe in order to accommodate the massive powerplant. New induction, exhaust, and control systems were developed, and outer wing panels were strengthened to handle the extra loads. Goodyear engineers also cut down the aircraft's fuselage and adopted a free blown bubble canopy setup similar to those on the late model Republic P-47 Thunderbolts and North American P-51 Mustangs.

The F2G's fuel system consisted of one 235-gallon self-sealing tank, mounted in the fuselage between the engine and the cockpit firewall. There were also two 37.5-gallon outer wing tanks, a 65-gallon self-sealing fuselage tank behind the pilot's seat, and two optional 150-gallon external drop tanks hung on center section hard points. The main fuel tank was equipped with a 700-gallon per hour submerged centrifugal pump that served as a booster and emergency backup in the event of a master pump failure. It also had a built-in fuel agitator (eggbeater) that acted as a deaerating appara-

The 1946 Bendix Trophy Race featured 22 aircraft, including a lone Goodyear FG-1D Corsair, entered by owner Dave Weyler. Race Number 90 was painted white with blue trim. (Bowers Collection)

Goodyear F2G Production List

Designation	BuNo	GAC Fab. No.	No. Built	Description
XF2G-1	13471	480	1	GAC test aircraft for R-4360-4 engine. Long chord cowl; top deck carburetor air intake. Goodyear chrome-yellow cowl, No. 5.
XF2G-1	13472	481	1	Same as above
XF2G-1	14691 – 14695	1700 – 1704	5	First true F2G; long cord cowl, top deck carburetor air intake, increased vertical fin area, split rudder, and bubble canopy.
F2G-1	88454 – 88458	1 – 5	5	Production aircraft, same configuration as GAC Fab. No. 1700 through 1704. Land based fighter.
F2G-2	88459 – 88463	6 – 10	5	Production aircraft, same F2G-1 except arrestor and catapult hook. Carrier based fighter.

While searching through the Navy's Aircraft History Cards, the authors discovered the possibility of one additional XF2G-1. According to this particular aircraft's history card, it was originally delivered to Navy Squadron VF-84 as a Goodyear FG-1, BuNo 14591. There is no indication of when this aircraft was modified, but the second page of the history card clearly indicates that BuNo 14591 ended its Navy career as an XF2G-1 on December 31, 1945. It should be noted that Goodyear's Flight Test department did contribute nine aircraft to the F2G development program. The authors developed this information from the Goodyear document "Weekly Summary Report of Flight Engineering Activity" of various dates (specifically see October 30, 1944, and November 20, 1944). These nine aircraft (the eight known aircraft are: BuNos 12992, 13007, 13374, 13703, 14062, 14091, 14092, and Royal Navy Corsair KD554) received certain F2G modifications, but were never fully converted and did not bear the XF2G designation. Thus, BuNo14591 could be the ninth Goodyear flight test aircraft that, simply through a clerical error, was given the XF2G designation by mistake. (Production List courtesy of Betty Olinger.)

tus, which helped remove suspended air in the fuel, reducing the threat of vapor lock. To take advantage of this air-removing device, all of the F2G's fuel was transferred to the main tank before it was delivered to the engine.

The F2G's oil system was a conventional type, incorporating oil coolers arranged in parallel flow, and engine-driven pressure and scavenge pumps fed by a 26.6-gallon oil tank mounted on the upper section of the firewall. Early in the XF2G flight test program it was discovered that a new lubrication strategy was needed for the R-4360 engine. During simulated combat tests, the F2G's oil pressure indicator would drop to zero after any change in attitude that resulted in negative g-loads on the airplane. The problem was traced to oil in a line that was placed near the bottom of the oil tank. When the aircraft was put into a negative 'g' attitude, oil would gravitate to the top of the container, leaving little reserve for the engine. Therefore, Goodyear set about redesigning the airplane's conventional lubrication scheme, and replaced it with what they called the "maneuver lubrication system."

The maneuver lubrication system consisted of an oil tank with both a main and a negative-load oil outlet. This system automatically switched between the main oil discharge aperture, which was used during its normal flight, and the negative oil passage opening during inverted maneuvers. Goodyear accomplished this feat by connecting the negative oil load outlet to a standpipe extending to an assigned level inside the oil tank. Both the main and the negative oil outlets were coupled to a solenoid-operated diverter valve that was subsequently operated by a gravity-controlled switch. In effect, the sliding weight in the inertia switch would actuate the solenoid

Above: *Owner Dave Weyler enlisted Thomas F. Call, a former operations officer with the Sixth Air Force, to fly his Corsair in the 1946 Bendix. Call was not very familiar with the Corsair, but had no real problem in flying the aircraft. The standard military-configured Corsair with centerline mounted drop tank had a maximum range of approximately 1,500 miles. This was far short of 2,048 miles from Van Nuys, California, to Cleveland, Ohio. To make up for the mileage difference, Weyler reduced the weight of the former fighter and developed a race strategy of leaning out the fuel mixture as much as possible once the aircraft reached it race altitude.* (U.S. Navy)

diverter valve when the F2G is put into negative acceleration. Oil is then supplied from the inverted flight pick-up in the oil tank instead of the standard pick-up located in the bottom of the oil receptacle.

To give the aircraft increased directional control for carrier landings and wave-offs, a new auxiliary rudder was installed. It operated in two positions, neutral and 12.5 degrees to starboard. During high speed or maneuvering, the extra rudder remains fixed; however, when the wing flaps are lowered to any setting greater than 30 degrees, the rudder is fully deployed to the starboard position.

The Navy ordered 418 Goodyear F2Gs in 1944, but that number was reduced to 63 due to a material shortage. Goodyear's F2G developmental and productions programs were further cut shortly after V-E day to include only seven experimental XF2Gs and 10 production aircraft broken down into equal groups of F2G-1s and F2G-2s. By

late 1949 all of the Navy's Goodyear F2Gs had been retired from service and stricken from its inventory.

In 1946 Frederick Crawford, president of Thompson Products, announced that the city of Cleveland, Ohio, after a six-year hiatus, would once again host the National Air Races during Labor Day weekend. Prior to World War II, the Cleveland National Air Races attracted large crowds of spectators and garnered national media attention that was perhaps only exceeded by the Indianapolis 500 motorcar race. Many of the young pilots who had recently returned from overseas war duty viewed the Crawford proclamation as an opportunity to capture the fame and wealth that had been bestowed upon the likes of Jimmy Doolittle and Roscoe Turner during air racing's Golden Age (1929–1939).

Simultaneously, the U.S. government began a program to sell many of the World War II aircraft types that were being stored at vari-

ous surplus yards around the country. Prospective race competitors flocked to these surplus sales depots to pick out the steed that would possibly capture one of the large cash prizes that were being offered by the sponsors of the racing events. Most of the future race pilots bought former Army Air Force fighters like the P-38 or the P-51; however, in 1946 two pilot-owners chose variants of the Vought F4U Corsair as their racer of choice.

During the summer of 1946, the National Air Race committee received 146 letters from pilots and owners who aspired to compete in the Labor Day classic. Returning as a major sponsor of the National Air Races was the Bendix Corporation. Malcolm P. Ferguson, president of the company, carrying on the tradition started by the late Vincent Bendix in 1929, once again put up the $24,000 in prize money for the Bendix Trophy Race.

The rules for this race were fairly simple, in that all the competing aircraft were to be equipped for instrument flight and the pilots had to hold an instrument rating. At noon, August 29, 1946, all of the Bendix entries were impounded on the ramp at Van Nuys Airport. Appearing on the hardstand that day were four North American P-51 Mustangs, 10 Lockheed P-38 Lightnings, one Douglas A-26 Invader, two Bell P-63 Kingcobras and one Goodyear FG-1D Corsair.

The Corsair was owned by 34 year-old David Weyler of Los Angeles. Weyler had only purchased the aircraft the month before and he hurriedly recruited Thomas F. Call, a former Sixth Air Force operations officer, to be the competing pilot. Call's Air Force background gave him little, if any, time in the Corsair, but he found the airplane to be easy to fly; however, its fuel consumption was somewhat high for a long-dis-

tance racer. Unfortunately, there was little time to modify the Goodyear fighter to carry extra fuel internally, but Weyler did attach a standard 172-gallon external drop tank to the centerline of the airplane.

More than 15,000 people crowded the Van Nuys Airport to witness the start of the first postwar Bendix event on morning of August 30, 1946. Twenty-two aircraft lined up to take off at three-minute intervals, and leading the pack was Thomas Call in his white and blue trimmed FG-1D. The lone Corsair displayed the Race Number 90 and had the name "Joe" painted on both sides of the fuselage.

Entrants devoted a considerable amount of time to increasing the performance of their machines while strategizing the flight plan that would deliver the fastest time over the 2,048 miles from Van Nuys to

Cleveland. Paul Mantz and his wet wing P-51C were the early odds-on favorite, followed by Jackie Cochran in her Irish green C-model Mustang. At 7:27 A.M., movie and recording star Dick Powell dropped the starting flag. Thomas Call let off the brakes and felt the g-forces push his body back into the seat as his Corsair leaped down the runway. After rotation, Call's racer rapidly climbed to approximately 35,000 feet, where he then leaned out the fuel mixture as much as possible. His idea was to stretch the fuel enough to fly nonstop, but it did not work as well as he had hoped. The main fuel tanks went dry about 10 minutes ahead of schedule, so Call decided to land at the Toledo Airport rather than risk a possible forced landing at Cleveland. Unfortunately, it took more than an hour to refuel the Corsair and the delay put him out of the race. Call did eventually make it to Cleveland, 1 1/2 hours behind Paul Mantz's winning bright red Mustang.

David Weyler, undaunted by his bad luck in 1946, once again entered his Corsair in the 1947 Bendix Trophy Race, and signed on Frank P. Whitton, a Marine Corps Reserve pilot, to fly the Goodyear racer for him. Also returning in 1947 was defending champion Paul Mantz, who once again was the odds-on favorite to capture the $10,000 first-place prize money. Among the 12 entries was also a highly modified Lockheed P-38F that was sponsored by Texas oil and hotel magnate Glen McCarthy. The hotelier was so confident that his gas-laden Lightning, named the *Flying Shamrock*, would win the Bendix that he placed a side bet with Mantz for an additional $10,000.

All the pre-race posturing soon faded away as Jane Page Hlavacek was flagged to start the cross-country race at 4:36 A.M., on the morning of August 30, 1947. One by one the

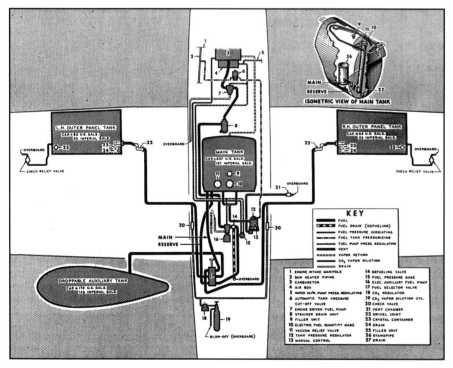

Schematic layout of a standard Corsair fuel system. The centerline external fuel tank added 172 gallons of fuel for the 2,048-mile trip. Call began to run low on fuel about 100 miles west of Cleveland, so he decided to refuel at Toledo before continuing the race. Unfortunately, the stop added more than an hour to Call's total elapsed time. (U.S. Navy)

racers took to the air, and then it came time for McCarthy's P-38 to take off. The plane seemed to strain at the weight of the four external fuel tanks as it rotated into the air. Then suddenly, the starboard tip tank fell off and burst into flames as it hit the ground. Pilot James Rubel continued on with the race in spite of the mishap, only to bail out after his aircraft caught fire over Arizona. Paul Mantz would go on to win his second Bendix Trophy, collecting $20,000 for his efforts.

Frank Whitton landed his Corsair at Cleveland Hopkins Airport six hours, 24 minutes and four seconds after taking off from Van Nuys. Few details exist concerning Whitton's race strategy or what may have transpired over the course of the trip, but it took him six minutes longer than it had taken Thomas Call to complete the race with an hour delay in 1946. Whitton still managed to win $500 for a seventh-place finish behind six P-51 Mustangs. The results of the 1947 Bendix Trophy Race proved once again that Weyler's basic FG-1D was no match for nonstop flying P-51s, and that fact alone effectively ended the Corsair's career as a Bendix racer.

1946 THOMPSON TROPHY RACE

The second part of the 1946 Cleveland National Air Races featured four days of pylon competitions, which were preceded by several days of practice and qualifying. Entered in the race was almost every type of aircraft that had served with the Army Air Force during World War II, plus one lone Goodyear Corsair that was owned by local favorite Cook Cleland. In addition to being a Cleveland native, Cleland is a war hero of some distinction.

He joined the Navy in 1940, and after flight training was attached to

Famed aviatrix Jackie Cochran and her Kelly Green P-51B finished the 1946 Bendix in second place, behind Paul Mantz. At the time, Cochran was lobbying the U.S. government to create a strong and coequal Air Force. (Bowers Collection)

a Vought SB2U Vindicator squadron on the USS *Wasp* (CV-7). The *Wasp* was patrolling the Atlantic when the Japanese sank the USS *Lexington* (CV-2) during the Battle of Coral Sea. *Wasp* was then recalled to the United States to be refitted and was subsequently deployed to the Pacific, where ironically the Japanese sank it as well. Cleland, along with many of his shipmates, was told to abandon ship, so he swam to a raft and was rescued just before dark by a destroyer. He was later assigned to the new USS *Lexington* (CV-16), where he spent the next two years flying Douglas SBD dive-bombers. During his combat tour, Cleland managed to shoot down five enemy planes, and helped sink a Japanese aircraft carrier with a 1,000-pound bomb. His wartime accomplishments earned him the Navy Cross, the Air Medal with three stars, and a Purple Heart.

In 1946, Cook Cleland purchased a Goodyear FG-1D Corsair from the War Assets Administration for $1,250, and he managed to get Goodyear Aircraft in Akron, Ohio, to help get the plane ready for the

National Air Races. He went on to qualify his white and maroon Corsair for the Thompson Trophy Race with an average speed of 361.809 mph.

The competition for the 1946 Thompson was formidable indeed. Bell Aircraft Co. test pilot Tex Johnston flew his hopped-up P-39 Airacobra around the practice course at a blazing speed of 409 mph. Johnston was followed by George Welch, one of the first American pilots to engage the Japanese at Pearl Harbor. Welch qualified in a black Mustang that had been tricked out by technicians from North American Aviation. Qualifying third was Chuck Tucker's P-63, which had so little wing area that it hardly looked like it would fly. The last plane to qualify ahead of Cleland was pre-war race veteran Tony LeVier in his bright red Lockheed P-38 Lightning.

On September 2, 1946, all 12 of the Thompson Trophy competitors lined up for the racehorse start. Cle-

Left: *Paul Mantz extended the range of his P-51C by wetting the wings of his racer. This approach increased the aircraft's interior fuel capacity to 856 gallons, as compared to the Mustang's normal internal fuel load of 269 gallons.* (Bowers Collection)

Right: *Mantz pushed his Mustang to its limits by running the engine at 3,000 rpm while pulling 67 inches of manifold. In the end, this race strategy brought Mantz the first of three postwar Bendix Trophy victories.* (H.G. Martin Photo from the Robert Collection, via Kansas Aviation Museum—Pickett-KAM)

land was flanked on the left by Tony LeVier and on the right by Steve Wittman's P-63. The deafening sound of 13 engines running at full take-off power could be heard around the airport as the starting flag dropped. Tex Johnston's P-39 *Cobra II* was the first off the ground, but was closely followed by Chuck Tucker's clipped wing P-63. Unfortunately, Tucker could not retract his landing gear, so he was the first to depart the course, with George Welch moving into second place. During the second lap, Welch, too, was forced to leave the race with engine trouble. LeVier's P-38 kept in sight of *Cobra II*, while three Mustangs passed Cook Cleland's Corsair. *Cobra II* continued to lead the race with plenty of power to spare. Every time LeVier would try to make up ground, Johnston would just give his P-39's Allison engine a little more fuel. In the end, Johnston's yellow and black *Cobra II* easily won the 1946 Thompson Trophy Race. Cleland managed to win $1,500 for a sixth-place finish, but the experience showed him that his Corsair did not have enough horsepower to capture the big money.

1947: Enter the F2G

In 1947, Cook Cleland approached his old friend Admiral William "Bull" Halsey and convinced him that the Navy's honor was at stake in the National Air Races. Cleland went on to tell Halsey that he could defend Naval Aviation and win the prestigious Thompson Trophy if he was allowed to buy one of Navy's Goodyear F2G Corsairs. Halsey liked the idea and arranged for Cleland to get his airplane.

Cleland bought three surplus F2Gs (one each XF2G-1, F2G-1 and F2G-2). Both the XF2G-1 (BuNo 14693) and F2G-2 (BuNo 88463) were modified at the Vought factory in Stratford, Connecticut. Each aircraft was made lighter by removing the armor plating, wing folding mechanisms (F2G-2), tail hook, and radio

Local hero Cook Cleland piloted the one and only FG-1D Corsair to enter the 1946 Thompson Trophy Race. Cleland qualified Lucky Gallon *in sixth position with an average speed of 361.809 mph.* (Bowers Collection)

equipment. The tail wheel was also replaced with a completely retractable wheel. Two feet was removed from the wingspan of each racer when the production wing tips were replaced with streamlined balsa wood versions. The typical F2G split rudder tail assemblies were also replaced with a standard F4U vertical stabilizers. The overall aerodynamic characteristics were improved by sealing up the gun ports. The fuel consumption for the F2G was very high, and the standard aircraft did not carry enough fuel for a 300-mile race, so two special tanks were installed in the fuselage behind the pilot's seat. One was for additional fuel while the other held 100 gallons of water for the water injection system. Lastly, both racers were fitted with specially thinned Hamilton Standard propellers.

Cleland could not afford to adorn his F2G-1 with the vast number of improvements that were accomplished by the Vought workers, so he decided to prepare the aircraft for Bendix Racing instead. The pilot he selected for this race was his best friend and partner, Dick Becker.

The thirsty 28-cylinder "corn cob" engine would need additional fuel, so Cleland and Becker increased the airplane's fuel capacity by adding external drop tanks. Cleland also arranged to lease a 350-acre farm in Missouri, so Becker would have a place to drop the empty fuel containers before making the final all-out push to Cleveland. Unfortunately, the Civil Aeronautics Administration (CAA) had rules against dropping items from an airplane, and would not grant Cleland a special dispensation for the Bendix. Cleland set aside the idea of competing in the Bendix and focused on entering the F2G-1 in the pylon events at Cleveland. Pilot Tony Janazzo made a deal with Cleland to pilot the plane with the hope of earning money to further his dream of getting into the medical profession.

Meanwhile a young navy test pilot named Ron Puckett also bought his way into the F2G game. Puckett was stationed at Naval Air Test Center (NATC) Patuxent River, Maryland, when he drove down to the War Assets office in Washington, D.C., and purchased, with some dif-

ficulty, a Goodyear XF2G-1. It took a little while for the paperwork to get to the Navy, so Puckett used that time, and the Navy's oil and fuel, to break in the airplane's low-time engine. Later he set about converting the Navy fighter into a racing plane by removing military equipment and systems to save weight. During the war, Puckett had served with a Grumman F6F Hellcat squadron and was credited with four kills. Every once in awhile, he would get into mock dogfights with Corsairs from a sister squadron, and during these engagements he noticed that vapor would form at the tips of the Corsair's wings, which did not happen with the Hellcat. Puckett figured that something must have been going on with the Corsair's tips, so he removed them from his XF2G-1 and substituted balsa wood versions, patterned from the Hellcat.

Word got around the country that no fewer than four mighty "Hose Nose" Goodyear Corsairs would compete in the 1947 National Air Races. Many of the returning competitors quickly realized that

George Welch was one of the few pilots who managed to get into the air during the attack on Pearl Harbor in 1941. After the war, North American Aviation (NAA) hired Welch as a test pilot. The P-51D he piloted in the 1946 Thompson was not officially sponsored by NAA, but was the odds-on favorite to win the 300-mile race. Unfortunately, an engine failure in lap two ended Welch's racing career. (David Ostrowski Collection)

The wings on Chuck Tucker's Bell P-63 barely looked long enough to support the aircraft. Pre-race publicity claimed that the racer was capable of more than 600 mph. Tucker's qualifying speed of 392.157 mph captured the fourth position. In the Thompson, Tucker's sleek racer was among the first to become airborne, but he could not retract his landing gear and was forced to leave the race in lap one. (Bowers Collection)

the F2Gs were the airplanes to beat after seeing Cook Cleland and Dick Becker post the two highest qualifying speeds. Puckett did not have the resources or sponsors afforded to Cleland, but he managed to qualify seventh, which was behind Cleland's third Corsair, piloted by Tony Janazzo. At 23, Janazzo was the youngest pilot to qualify for the 1947 Thompson.

As the qualifying rounds came to an end, the weather replaced the National Air Races as the major newsmaker in Cleveland area. On Saturday, August 30, 1947, severe thunderstorms, accompanied by high winds and heavy rains, lashed Cleveland and the surrounding areas. This forced the National Air Race Committee to cancel most of the scheduled events for the day. Only 6,000 people showed up to

watch Paul Mantz win his second consecutive Bendix Trophy Race when he touched down his bright red P-51C on the rain-soaked field. In order to compensate for lost time, air race officials decided to combine Saturday's attractions with those that had already been scheduled for the following two days. This decision would especially affect the 1947 Thompson Trophy Race, which many consider the wildest air competition in postwar National Air Race history.

1947 THOMPSON TROPHY RACE

In 1946, the rules allowed aircraft of various types to compete with each other in all of the racing events. This unlimited format, unfortunately, produced lopsided victories that tended to bore the spectators. The producers of the National Air Races decided in 1947 to handicap all the pylon events, with the exception of the Thompson. The Sohio Trophy Race was limited

to Lockheed P-38s, the Kendall featured P-51s, and lastly, only P-63s were allowed to compete in the Tinnerman Trophy Race.

Labor Day Monday was the last day of the 1947 Nationals, and on this day the officials scheduled the Tinnerman race that was closely followed by the all-important Thompson. William Bour, the only P-63 pilot to qualify for both events, informed officials that he fully intended to fly in each race. This meant that Bour, in the span of about 13 minutes, would have to land after competing in the Tinnerman, fuel his A-model P-63, and then get in the starting lineup. Race officials were concerned that they would not have 12 aircraft for the race so they asked Jean "Skip" Ziegler to act as an alternate, in case Bour did not make it. This was a somewhat unorthodox request, because Ziegler's Curtiss XP-40Q had not qualified to race in the Thompson.

Bour came in dead last in the Tinnerman, and while he getting his airplane ready for the next race the other aircraft were lining up. Cook Cleland got his F2G-1 (Race Number 74) stuck in the mud and for a while it looked like the front-runner might miss the event as well. Fortunately, Jay Demming and others sent crews over to help and soon Cleland was at his starting position. All 12 pilots trained their eyes on the starting flag as their aircraft, running at full throttle, pushed the limits of the brakes. Ron Puckett was the single exception, because he could not get his big R-4360 to run. William Bour pulled his P-63 alongside Charles Walling's modified P-38 Lightning just as the starter dropped the flag. A sudden rush of aircraft raced ahead of Puckett, who was still struggling with his engine. The starter, seeing Puckett's situa-

Bill Odom entered an R-2800-powered Republic YP-47M-1 in 1947. The aircraft was laden with fuel when it sprung a leak just before the start of the 1947 Bendix, and Odom wisely decided not to compete in the event. (Bowers Collection)

tion, quickly waived Ziegler's P-40Q to enter the race. (It is important to note that today some confusion still exists over Ziegler's entry in the 1947 Thompson event. Some have even suggested Skip Ziegler somehow illegally pushed his way into the race. This is simply not true. His entry in the 1947 Thompson Trophy event was completely legal and sanctioned by the governing air race officials.)

Jay Demming's P-39 *Cobra II* was the first racer in the air. As Cleland became airborne he realized the he had airplanes all around him, so he got as low and as close to the scatter pylon as possible. He was so low, in fact, that his aircraft brushed some of the trees as he gained speed. During the first lap Jack Hardwick's P-51C blew its engine, and he was forced to make a spectacular emergency landing. Fortunately, Hardwick was able to escape from the burning plane. (Legend has it that Hardwick had his racer insured for $25,000 and when the fire trucks arrived, he told the firemen to let it burn. Over the years some race historians have jokingly speculated that Jack Hardwick, in spite of his crash, was the real big money winner at Cleveland in 1947.) In the interim, Puckett finally got his big Corsair started and entered the race during the second lap, while Walling departed the course and landed his rough-running P-38.

Cleland trailed both Dick Becker and Jay Demming for two laps around the parallelogram-shaped 30-mile course. Then Cleland poured the fuel to his R-4360 and passed *Cobra II,* but failed to jump ahead of his good friend Becker. During the next lap Cleland gained a little altitude while he kept up the pressure on Becker's XF2G-1 (race 94). He then converted his extra altitude into speed as he dove past

Bell test pilot Tex Johnston was the top qualifier at Cleveland, and he also easily won the 1946 Thompson Trophy Race with an average speed of 373.908 mph. Along with the trophy came $15,000 in prize money. (Pickett-KAM)

Becker in the red and white Race Number 94. During the seventh lap, Tony Janazzo and his black Super Corsair appeared to be in trouble as it weaved past pylon 2. Instead of turning as it should have, Janazzo's F2G-2 kept flying straight for about two miles before striking the earth. A later autopsy showed that Janazzo's blood was full of carbon monoxide. The Corsair was notorious for allowing the deadly gas to creep into the cockpit, and before the race Cleland and Becker had tried, to no avail, to get Janazzo to use an oxygen mask.

As the race continued, Paul Penrose, flying the same Mustang that failed George Welch in 1946, left the racecourse in the eighth lap with a sick airplane. Penrose at one point

had been in third place behind Becker and Cleland and posted laps of more than 400 mph. However, in the end, his Rolls-Royce Merlin could not take the stress.

Cleland was clearly in the lead by the 10th lap, and now the real competition was for second place. Dick Becker continued to fly a fast and steady course, but Jay Demming's P-39 pressed him hard. Spectators on the ground could only view the racers for a few seconds as they passed the grandstands, and it was difficult for them to see who was winning. This confusion became more acute when the faster planes began to lap the slower ones. Woody Edmondson, who, at 34, was the oldest pilot in the race, began to have engine trouble during lap 11.

A dapper-looking Cook Cleland posing for a publicity photo in his red and white Corsair named Lucky Gallon. *(Burke-Smith Studios)*

Lucky Gallon *was the only radial engine aircraft to compete in the 1946 Thompson. After the race, Cleland was not satisfied with his sixth place finish. He realized that he would need more horsepower to win in 1947. (Burke-Smith Studios)*

Suddenly the Allison engine in his North American A-36A blew up as he turned pylon three on the backside of the course. Edmondson put his ailing aircraft down in a field and walked away from the crash with his life. Three laps later Ziegler's engine also quit. Fortunately, he had enough air speed to gain some altitude and pointed the aircraft away from the crowds before the experimental XP-40Q began to stall. He then bailed out of his racer, and broke his right leg upon landing in a railroad yard near the Cleveland Hopkins Airport.

Cleland's Corsair continued to lead the strung-out pack of racers. Ron Puckett, although he was still a lap down, passed Steve Beville's P-51 *Galloping Ghost* to move into fourth place behind Cleland, Becker, and Demming. During the 19th lap, Puckett engaged the blower without making the mixture rich enough, and his engine backfired, blowing

off the air scoop. In the final lap, Jay Demming attempted to pass Dick Becker's red and white corsair, but Becker managed to hold him off and finished second.

The Cleland-Becker racing team won a total of $27,600, but it was a bittersweet victory as they had also lost one of their comrades in the competition. Out of the 13 planes that started the 1947 Thompson, only six finished the 300-mile, 20-lap race. Incidentally, Bill Bour finished last, as he had in the Tinnerman.

1948: CLELAND AND BECKER'S YEAR OF EXPERIMENTATION

In 1947, Cleland and Becker clearly established that their powerful Goodyear F2Gs were the machines to beat, and they fully expected to run the field again in 1948. In addition, Cleland had a "secret weapon" in the form of a new fuel called Methyl Triptane.

The Shell Oil Company, which claimed its performance number was between 200 and 300, developed Methyl Triptane or 2,2,3 trimethyl butane. This meant that the new fuel would allow race pilots to pull higher manifold pressures than if they were using the same amount of 100-octane gas. Cleland and Becker, along with approximately 10 other racing teams, decided to try this fuel. Testing during the first few days of qualifying, when the sky was clear and the air temperature was warm, suggested the new fuel did give the Corsairs a performance boost. In spite of the perceived advantage of the new fuel, Chuck Brown, the third pilot to compete in Tex Johnston's former P-39 *Cobra II*, claimed the pole position in the Thompson with a new record speed of 418.300 mph. Cleland was close behind at 417.424 mph, and Becker's race 74 was clocked at 405.882 mph.

Absent from qualifying for the races in 1948 was Ron Puckett's Corsair. Puckett had a friend fly his airplane to Cleveland and, for reasons that are still unknown, this pilot used the XF2G-1's emergency gear extension system to blow the wheels down during a routine landing. Unfortunately, Puckett was unable to fix the Corsair's locked down

landing gear in time to qualify for the racing events.

On the afternoon of Sunday, September 6, 1948, 10 racers lined the field, ready to leap into the air from the racehorse start. When the flag was dropped, there was a scramble for the scatter pylon. The tremendous torque of Brown's P-39 forced the aircraft to the left side of the first pylon. Brown corrected his path by rolling the aircraft to the right and managed to gain the inside position on the two Corsairs and never looked back. By the second lap his P-39 was approximately a mile ahead of Cleland, and was averaging a record speed of 413 mph. Dick Becker experienced a massive engine backfire in the third lap that dislodged his cowling. This condition forced Becker to leave the race. Two laps later, the same thing happened Cleland's XF2G-1, and he was also forced to return to the airport. With the two Corsairs gone, Brown figured he had the race won. Bob Eucker's P-63 was the next to drop out in the sixth lap. The P-51s flown by M.W. Fairbrother and Woody Edmundson also experi-

Dave Weyler again entered his Corsair in the 1947 Bendix competition. Weyler's new pilot, Frank Whitton, flew the distance to Cleveland in six hours, 24 minutes, and four seconds, fast enough to take sixth place in the cross-country event. (Logan Coombs)

enced failures in the 13th and 14th laps respectively. In the meantime, Chuck Brown continued to lead the four remaining competitors until his engine quit in the 19th lap. This allowed Anson Johnson, a 24 year-old airline pilot, to win the 1948 Thompson in basically a stock P-51D Mustang. Bruce Raymond's Mustang and Wilson Newhall's P-63 followed Johnson.

Post-race analysis showed that the Triptane, burning more slowly, was not finished burning when fresh fuel was introduced into the combustion chamber, causing a backfire. The failure in Chuck Brown's P-39 was attributed to a small piece of cowling that departed the plane during the race. This exposed the carburetor fuel line to heat from the engine's exhaust gases, producing vapor bubbles in the gasoline. The engine would momentarily cut out every time a bubble reached the throat of the carburetor, and by the 19th lap the line apparently became hot enough to produce a total vapor lock.

1949: Victory Above Tragedy

The previous year's formula for the National Air Races had failed to produce the type of competition the Air Racing Association desired, so in 1949 officials again adjusted the format. For safety reasons, the Thompson was shortened from 300 to 225 miles. A shorter course meant the racers could carry less fuel and water, and that translated into less wing loading in the turns. It also

One of the expected front-runners in 1947 was James Ruble's modified Lockheed P-38F Lightning. The Flying Shamrock *was sponsored by hotel and oil magnate Glen McCarthy, who had a $10,000 side bet with 1946 winner Paul Mantz. The right wing tank departed the heavily loaded Lightning not long after Rubel became airborne. Fire in the engine nacelle later forced Rubel to bail out of the aircraft over Arizona.* (Bowers Collection)

Below: *Paul Mantz won his second Bendix Trophy in 1947. The actual event had been canceled in Cleveland due to severe weather, but Mantz and many of his competitors managed to land at Hopkins Airport anyway.* (Bowers Collection)

Above Right: *Jack Hardwick's P-51C was the first casualty of the 1947 Thompson. He departed the course in the first lap and shortly thereafter survived a horrific crash landing. Hardwick reportedly had his racer insured for $25,000, which prompted many air race historians to crown him the true winner (at least in terms of money) of the 1947 Thompson.* (Logan Coombs)

offered the F2G pilots the possibility of lessening the load in the aft compartment, which had made some the aircraft difficult to fly in the early laps of the race.

The four-sided course itself was revamped into a seven-segment track that was almost circular. The modified course had shorter straightaways and seven turns, and

the angle between each section of the race path was less than 90 degrees. This meant that the g-loads on the plane and pilot would be less than the previous year's course, with its four very sharp turns.

In 1949, four F2Gs once again graced the competition. Cook Cleland and Dick Becker were back, along with their partner, Ben

McKillen. Also returning was Ron Puckett. After their disappointing 1948 race campaign, both Cleland and Puckett further modified their racers during the year's long hiatus. Puckett removed the extra rudder assembly from his Corsair and installed a thinned-down propeller that he claimed improved his top speed by 20 knots. Cleland took a more radical approach with his white racer, number 94, removing approximately eight feet of wing surface, and capping the end of each outer panel with a wing plate.

Cleland and Puckett's mighty R-4360-powered Corsairs did not garner all of the pre-race media attention, because of two highly modified P-51 Mustangs that looked very fast. Anson Johnson, not satisfied with his lucky win in 1948, returned to Cleveland with a bright yellow, highly modified P-51. In 1948, he had improved the performance of his stock Mustang by installing a water-injected Rolls-Royce Merlin V-1650-25 engine, so the next step was to make his racer more aerodynamically efficient. To this end he removed the Mustang's

Cook Cleland's friend Dick Becker piloted Race Number 94. The red and white racer sported clipped wings in addition to a homemade air intake that extended to the edge of the engine cowling. This simple modification provided additional ram air to the engine and helped boost the motor's overall horsepower. (Logan Coombs)

belly scoop and replaced the standard coolant radiator with modified Bell P-39 type radiators, installed in leading edges of the main wings. A system of ductwork vented the cooling air to a negative pressure area on the upper side of the wing. The other Mustang that attracted the attention of race fans was the infamous P-51 named *Beguine.*

Beguine was the brainchild of Walter Beech, who in early 1948 came up with an idea for a P-51 racer with asymmetric wings. He figured that having the left wing shorter than the right would help a racing airplane turn the pylons faster. He assigned the task of creating such a craft to his good friend J.D. Reed, the leading Beechcraft distributor in the country. Reed purchased a C-model Mustang and sent it to California to be modified by North American Aviation engineers and technicians. They followed Anson Johnson's approach, removing the stock cooling system and locating replacement radiators in nacelles or pods on the wingtips. One side was used to exchange heat from the engine's coolant, while the other cooled the oil. The aircraft also sported a specially thinned Hamilton-Standard propeller. All of the aircraft's surfaces were perfectly finished, painted an emerald green, and polished to a high luster.

Ten days before the start of the 1949 Nationals, J.D. Reed and Walter Beech sold the beautiful *Beguine* to Jackie Cochran's husband, Floyd Odlum. Cochran, in a surprise move, then selected William P. "Bill" Odom to be its pilot. Odom had made a name for himself by breaking the round-the-world speed record in both 1947 and 1948. He also piloted a modified Beechcraft Bonanza nonstop from Hawaii to Teterboro, New Jersey; however, he had no experience in pylon racing

Cook Cleland entered a third F2G in the Thompson, but was not financially able to give Race Number 84 the thinned-down propeller that adorned his other two racers. According to Dick Becker, this particular aircraft was painted black because it was the cheapest paint they could find. Tony Janazzo piloted number 84, and at 23 years old was the youngest pilot to qualify for the Thompson. During the race Janazzo was overcome by exhaust fumes and was killed when the airplane crashed in a field shortly after completing the sixth lap of the Thompson. (Pickett-KAM)

and very little, if any, in high-performance, fighter-type aircraft.

Cook Cleland qualified his modified XF2G-1 at 407.211 mph but failed to capture the pole position. That particular distinction went to his best friend and partner Dick

Becker, who posted a speed of 414.592 mph. Unfortunately, it was not Becker's year, for the engine in race 74 failed shortly after he finished his run. Becker was forced to make an emergency landing. Rookie race pilots Bill Odom, piloting the

Race Number 74 was the aircraft that Cook Cleland chose to enter at Cleveland in 1947. Vought Aircraft assisted Cleland in modifying the aircraft for the races by reducing its overall weight by approximately 1,000 pounds. Vought replaced the standard split rudder with a smaller F4U rudder. (Pickett-KAM)

Beguine, and Ben McKillen, flying Cleland's third F2G, rounded out the top four starting positions with respective speeds of 405.565 mph and 396.280 mph.

THE 1949 SOHIO AND TINNERMAN TROPHY RACES

On Saturday, September 3, 1949, nine aircraft started the Sohio Trophy Race, and rookie race pilot Bill Odom was at the pole. Odom's lack of experience did not appear to show, as he went on to easily win at an average speed of 388.393 mph. Ron Puckett's F2G *Miss Port Columbus* kept the pressure on Odom throughout the race. Puckett could have probably won if he had pushed it, but instead he decided to save his engine for the Thompson, coasting to a second-place finish.

The following day, Ben McKillen's Corsair approached the pole position for the Tinnerman competition as he waited for the starting flag to drop. Cleland had

The fourth F2G to enter the Thompson was owned and piloted by Ron Puckett. Puckett's Race Number 18 was painted dark blue with an orange cowling and tailcone. It had a standard cowling and a standard tail with split rudder, but was still a very fast racer. He qualified seventh with an average speed of 371.415 mph. Race Number 18 stalled at the start of the race, and Puckett was a lap down by the time he finally got airborne. Undaunted by the late start, Puckett began to gain ground on his competitors. In the 19th lap, Puckett was in fourth place when his engine quit. (Pickett-KAM)

managed to purchase this aircraft from the Navy with proviso that it was not to be flown. At some point before the races, Cleland and Becker

decided to attach the data plate that had come from Tony Janazzo's ill-fated F2G-1 to the grounded surplus Goodyear warbird, and they got it ready to fly. McKillen, a flight instructor at Cleland's air service, was not interested in incorporating the many race modifications that were applied to Cleland's other racers. Instead he insisted on keeping the F2G as close as possible to its original stock configuration. Ultimately, race 57's lack of racing refinements did not matter, because McKillen easily captured the checkered flag and won the Tinnerman Trophy Race.

THE 1949 THOMPSON

The Thompson Trophy Races had the biggest purse of all the pylon races. The winner of this competition would take home at least $16,000. Considering the average annual income in the United States in 1949 was approximately $2,000, it is no

Cleland borrowed an air scoop that had been developed by the U.S. Navy and Pratt & Whitney. This device allowed more air to reach the throat of the carburetor. The new scoop, when coupled with high-octane fuel, boosted the power of the R-4360 to more than 4,000 horsepower. Number 74 had a water tank and a fuel tank installed behind the pilot seat. The weight of these tanks shifted the F2G's center of gravity aft, which made the racer very difficult to fly during the early stages of the Thompson. (Pickett-KAM)

Below: *Bell test pilot Jay Demming took over piloting duties of* Cobra II *from Tex Johnston. Demming flew a very competitive race but narrowly lost the second place prize money to Dick Becker's F2G.* (Bell Aircraft via Jay Demming)

Above: *George Welsh's former P-51D was once again in the Thompson mix; however, in 1947 Paul Penrose was at the controls of the racer. Here Paul Penrose (right) is shown shaking hands with the aircraft owner, Ron Freeman.* (Burke-Smith Studios)

wonder that Cook Cleland, although he qualified for lesser events, saved all of his efforts for the big show.

The race itself was a showdown between the powerful Goodyear Corsairs of Cleland, McKillen, and Puckett, and the newly modified Mustangs of Johnson and Odom. McKillen was first off at the drop of the starter's flag, while the other contenders jockeyed for position. Puckett was the last to get airborne. McKillen led through the first lap but soon was overtaken by Cleland, who would never give up the lead.

Back in the pack, a duel em-

erged between the P-51s flown by Bill Odom, in *Beguine*, and Steve Beville piloting *Galloping Ghost*. Odom would pull alongside and look over at Beville as if to ask him to give way. But Beville was a true race competitor, and there was no way he was going to give up his position. Odom later pushed the stick forward and slipped under and out in front of Beville. As Odom approached pylon two, he banked sharply to the left, then slow-rolled back to the right. *Beguine* then went nose down and crashed into a house, killing a young woman and

her child. What actually happened in Odom's cockpit will never be known, but the late Steve Beville believed that Odom misjudged his line-up on the pylon and tried to correct it by rolling the plane to the right. Unfortunately, Odom did not maintain control of the *Beguine*.

Meanwhile, Cook Cleland continued to lead the race through eight laps while posting the fastest lap on each circuit. Ron Puckett then began to make his move and passed up all of his fellow competitors to get into second place behind Cleland's white Corsair. In the 12th lap, Cleland once

Skip Ziegler's P-40Q did not qualify for the Thompson, but the race officials allowed him to line up for the race as a alternate, because they were worried that Bill Bour's P-63 would not make the start. When Puckett stalled, the flagman motioned for Ziegler to enter the race. The P-40Q' s engine failed in lap 13, but Ziegler managed to pilot the Curtiss fighter over the grandstand before bailing out of the stricken craft. He survived the low-altitude jump, but broke his leg upon hitting the ground. (Bowers Collection)

again took total control of the race by posting four consecutive fastest laps and finishing the race for his second Thompson Trophy win. Puckett could have easily challenged Cleland's XF2G-1, but decided to cruise home with the sure winnings rather than possibly finishing out of the money with a broken airplane. Ben McKillen came in third, making it a Corsair sweep of the 1949 Thompson Trophy Race.

As for Anson Johnson, his highly modified Mustang was never a threat to any of the Goodyear-built Corsairs. He was never able to gain on any of the leaders and was forced to depart the course in the ninth lap, when some of the exhaust stacks departed his Merlin engine.

THE SUN SETS ON THE RACING F2G

No one knew it at the time, but 1949 was the last unlimited race to be held in Cleveland, Ohio. The fallout from the Odom accident and the start of the Korean War forced race officials to cancel the 1950 National Air Races. The world was a different place, and the end of the races at Cleveland was the end of an era.

Looking back more than 50 years later, it is obvious that the Pratt & Whitney R-4360 engine was well suited for the events of the Cleveland National Air Races. Some of the records that were established between 1946 and 1949 stood for approximately 20 years. Unfortunately, the F2Gs that accounted for the records during the postwar racing period did not fare as well. Ron Puckett's Race Number 84 eventually found its way to a salvage operation in Salisbury, Maryland. Today, all that remains of this aircraft is its data plate. The airframe of Cook Cleland's number 94 is buried in a

The Shell Oil Company introduced a new slow-burning fuel called Methyl Triptane-1 at Cleveland. Shell claimed that Triptane had a performance number of approximately 200/300. Cleland and Becker were among several racing teams to use the exotic fuel in 1948. (Bowers Collection)

Methyl Triptane proved to be Cleland's undoing in 1948. Although Cleland had tested the new fuel during the warm, sunny days of qualification, the day of the race it was overcast and cool, and when Cleland pushed the engine to 3,900 horsepower, it backfired and blew the scoop loose. (Burke-Smith Studios)

Dick Becker turning the home pylon after qualifying at 414.592 mph. Shortly thereafter Number 74's engine failed and put Becker on the sidelines for the duration of the races. (Pickett-KAM)

landfill on what is now NASA Lewis Research Center near Cleveland, Ohio. Walter Soplata saved number 74, and eventually sold the aircraft to the Crawford Museum. Ben McKillen's number 57 was derelict for a long time before being caught in the warbird craze of the 1970s. At that point number 57 bounced from one owner to the next before finally landing with Bob Odegaard, who restored the craft back to flying condition.

Below: *Ron Puckett reconfigured his F2G by replacing the split rudder with a standard Corsair type. He followed Cleland's lead and extended the carburetor air scoop to the edge of the engine's cowling for the 1949 races. (Burke-Smith Studios)*

Talk among the visitors at the Reno Air Races always includes terms that are in some way related to speed and power; however, in 1999 race fans had something new to add to their daily conversations. Namely, was Bob Odegaard going to bring his beautiful F2G to the races?

A rumor was circulating around the airport during the first few days of the 1999 National Championship Air Races that Bob Odegaard had entered his newly restored Goodyear F2G-1 Corsair in the Aviation Heritage Trophy competition. Each day a horde of press representatives and warbird enthusiasts made the trek to the far end of the ramp to see if the rumor had become fact. The anticipation and hope continued to grow as each day passed into history. Then late one afternoon, the bright red Super Corsair finally appeared over Stead Field.

Bob Odegaard acquired the former veteran of the 1949 Cleveland National Races in 1995 from Greg Morris, after the plane had been passed from Cook Cleland to Dick Becker, to John Trainor, to Harry Doan, to Don Knapp, and then to the Lone Star Flight Museum in Galveston, Texas. It was originally one of five production F2G-1s built by Goodyear Aircraft. This particular Corsair came along too late to record any significant military history; however, its civil history has spawned at least one mystery.

In 1947, Cook Cleland entered three surplus Goodyear F2G Corsairs in the Cleveland National Air Races. Cleland and Dick Becker would place first and second in the Thompson Trophy Race, but their partner, Tony Janazzo, wouldn't be so lucky. In the seventh lap, Janazzo's jet black Corsair plunged to earth at the edge of Hopkins Airport. Janazzo was not wearing an oxygen mask, and it was later discovered that he was overwhelmed by carbon monoxide fumes leaking into the cockpit from the big R-4360 engine. The aircraft he was flying that day carried the Navy Bureau of Aeronautics Number (BuNo) 88457 and civil registration of NX5588N. In 1949, Ben McKillen entered an F2G in the National Air Races, and his Corsair had the same BuNo and civil registration as Janazzo's F2G. Since 1949, many aviation historians have questioned whether or not the Janazzo and McKillen Corsairs were one in the

Cook Cleland, left, and Bob Odegaard at Reno 1999 with the Rolls-Royce Aviation Heritage Trophy and the F2G-1 formerly owned and raced by Cleland and his teammates, Dick Beck and Ben McKillen. Odegaard's restoration is of the highest quality, and Cleland's smile demonstrates his satisfaction in seeing the aircraft fly once again. (A. Kevin Grantham)

same. In 1997, Cook Cleland revealed why the two Corsairs had the same identification.

Sometime after the 1947 races, Cook Cleland bought a fourth F2G from the Navy, with a proviso that the plane would never be flown. (The exact date of the purchase and the identity of the aircraft are unknown.) Initially, Cleland was going to use the aircraft for spare parts. However, in 1949, he and his partners, Dick Becker and Ben McKillen, decided to again enter three Corsairs in the Cleveland racing events. They simply attached the data plate that came from Janazzo's ill-fated F2G to the McKillen Corsair. McKillen would go on to capture the 1949 Tinnerman Trophy Race, and

he placed third in the Thompson. While the true identity of the McKillen/Odegaard F2G may never be known, some historians believe the rare bird is the fifth production F2G-1, BuNo 88458.

Bob Odegaard has long been known for his beautiful Mustang restoration work, so it came as no surprise to most that his latest project would have the look of a winner. For two days, the five judges, including Tom Allison and William Reese from the Smithsonian's Paul Garber Facility, looked over the 15 aircraft entered in the Heritage competition. Each entry was judged on technical merit, authenticity, quality of workmanship, and attention to detail. When the bal-

lots were tallied, Odegaard's F2G was the overwhelming winner of both the Roll Royce Aviation Heritage Trophy and the Peoples' Choice Award. Presenting the trophies to Odegaard in a ceremony at Reno's show center, just after the completion of the Unlimited Gold Race, were Rolls Royce Vice President Chris Hornblower; National Air and Space Museum Acting Director Don Lopez; and astronaut James Lovell, a National Aviation Hall of Fame enshrinee.

In addition, a permanent trophy bearing Odegaard's name will be displayed at NAHF. In 2003, the permanent trophy will alternate between NAHF and the Smithsonian's new Dulles International Airport facility.

Bob Odegaard taxies out in F2G-1, Race Number 57, at Reno 1999. Ben McKillen won the Tinnerman Trophy Race and place third in the Thompson at Cleveland in 1949 in this aircraft. (A. Kevin Grantham)

Cook Cleland (left) and his best friend, Dick Becker. (Bruce Young Collection)

Sometime after the 1948 races, Cook Cleland decided to use a hydrogen peroxide injection system to boost more power from the R-4360, after reading some captured German reports on the subject. Cleland and Dick Becker experimented with different solutions but, in the end, the effects of the new injection formula had a negligible effect on the aircraft's top speed. (Logan Coombs)

Cochran's impressive looking Mustang was decorated with the music from the popular song "Begin the Beguine," which happened to be Jackie Reed's (J.D.'s wife) favorite song. (Earl Reinert)

The new emerald green Mustang was all the talk at Cleveland in 1949. This North American P-51C was originally modified for J.D. Reed on behalf of Walter Beech; however, it was sold to Jackie Cochran less than two weeks before the National Air Races. (Earl Reinert)

William P. Odom made a name for himself by breaking Howard Hughes' around-the-world speed record in 1947 and breaking his own record in 1948. However, Odom was not truly a qualified pylon race pilot and had very little time in the Beguine (background) when he entered the National Air Racing events. Many of his fellow race pilots felt that Odom's lack of experience contributed greatly to his fatal accident during the second lap of the 1949 Thompson Trophy Race. (Pickett-KAM)

The house located on West Street, Berea, Ohio, that fell victim to Bill Odom's fatal crash. A young mother and her infant child were also killed in the accident. This tragic event played a major role in putting an end to air racing in Cleveland for more than 20 years. (Ralph Willett)

Chuck Brown (left) and Cook Cleland (right) point to their respective qualifying speeds. Brown was the third pilot in three years to race Cobra II, and he managed to capture the pole position for the 1948 Thompson. (Bruce Young Collection)

Ben McKillen piloted Cook Cleland's third F2G. The aircraft itself was basically stock with the exception of added fuel and water tanks. (Bowers Collection)

The cloud formation in the early days of the 1949 National Air Races provided a photogenic backdrop for the photographers of the event. Here Ron Puckett is preparing his F2G for the upcoming qualification flight. (Pickett-KAM)

Race Number 18 was decorated in an attractive two-tone blue and was adorned as Miss Port Columbus. Puckett's racer also had a new propeller that was better suited for racing. The propeller change alone increased Puckett's top speed by approximately 20 knots. (Logan Coombs)

Cook Cleland passed Ben McKillen in the second lap of the Thompson Trophy Race and never looked back. His lead on the other flyers grew with each lap. Toward the end of the race, Cleland reduced his power and cruised across the finish line to capture his second Thompson Trophy and the prize money of $16,000. (Pickett-KAM)

RACEPLANE TECH
S E R I E S

A COMEBACK

Bill Odom's accident in the 1949 Thompson Trophy Race, while flying the highly modified P-51C *Beguine,* marked an end to Unlimited Air Racing in the United States for nearly 15 years. During the 1950s the sport of air racing was kept alive by a small number of intrepid souls who competed in homebuilt aircraft in races that were originally sponsored by the Goodyear Tire & Rubber Company. However, by 1960, interest in and sponsorship of air racing was peaking once again.

In late 1959, Bill Stead, former National Hydroplane Champion (1958 and 1959), made plans to revive the sport by holding the first annual National Championship Air Races at Sky Ranch near Reno, Nevada. Stead had been a big fan of the Cleveland races and often dreamed about holding and participating in such an event. In the early 1960s, Stead met Bob Hoover, and it was not long before the two pilots began promoting the revival of air racing. After many setbacks and dedicated campaigning by Stead and others in the Reno business community, the revival of the National Championship Air Races received a boost from the Nevada Centennial Year Commission. Nevada's governor at the time, Grant Sawyer, selected Stead to serve on the Centennial Commission. This gave the aviator and hydroplane racing champion the opportunity to campaign for Cleveland-style racing in the high desert outside Reno. The potential tourist draw of the races and Stead's enthusiasm sold the idea, and the Centennial Commis-

sion seeded the races with $40,000. The Sky Ranch airport was selected as the site for a number of reasons, one of which was that the Stead family owned the surrounding land, eliminating the possibility of com-

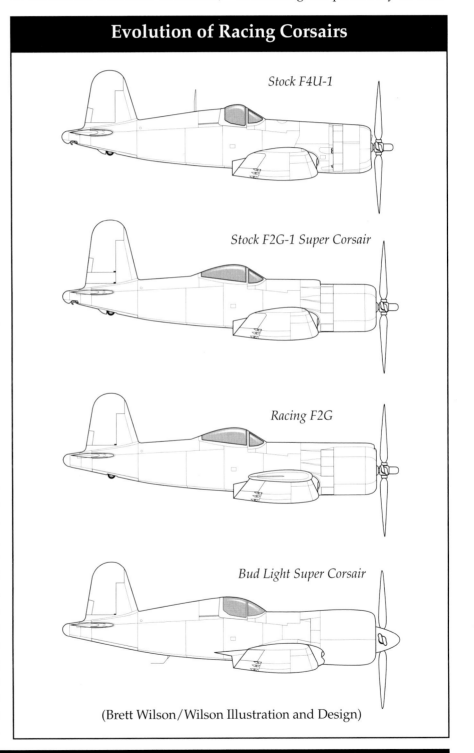

Evolution of Racing Corsairs

Stock F4U-1

Stock F2G-1 Super Corsair

Racing F2G

Bud Light Super Corsair

(Brett Wilson/Wilson Illustration and Design)

Gene Akers brought F4U-4 N6667, BuNo 97259, to Reno 1967 and qualified in the 10th position. Akers, a fire bomber pilot by trade, posted a qualifying speed of 315.098 mph. In the consolation race, Akers finished fourth out of six, finishing at an average speed of 300.78 mph. (Emil Strasser via Gerry Liang)

plaints from near-by residents. The Sky Ranch was rather crude in comparison to the polished airport setting of today's air races, and the lack of improvements forced a number of changes from the Cleveland racing model. Among them were eliminating the racehorse start, and instituting a point system similar to the one used in hydroplane racing.

All of the enthusiasm generated by the Reno races in 1964 saw a number of aviators turn their attention toward the revived sport. In addition to the Reno venue, the Los Angeles National Air Races, held at Fox Field, in Lancaster, California, got under way on Memorial Day weekend, May 29 to June 6, 1965. This race was the first Corsair

appearance in the modern era of air racing, and an FG-1D owned by Lou Kaufman was entered. Kaufman had tapped Lynn Whinney to fly the stock Goodyear-built fighter, Race Number 2 (N4719C, BuNo 92081) in competition. During a test hop before the competition, Whinney encountered problems while in the air. He was having trouble retracting the starboard landing gear, when he was last seen, heading west over the hills near Fox Field. The Corsair never returned to the field; it crashed, killing Whinney. Chuck Lyford went on to win the first Los Angeles National Air Races in his P-51D *Bardahl Special*.

It took another two years before a Corsair put in a sustained appearance around the pylons, and in 1967 spectators were treated to the sight of two Corsairs on the Reno ramp.

Gene Akers' F4U-4 (BuNo 97259, N6667) was the first bent-wing bird to arrive at Reno for the 1967 running of National Championship Air Races. Akers was a fire bomber pilot by trade, and his Corsair was sponsored by his employer, Cal-Nat Airways of Grass Valley, California. The aircraft was undergoing the conversion process from ex-Navy fighter to air racer and sat on the Reno ramp with its wings and fuselage bare metal while the cowl, rudder, and vertical were painted a deep green. "Race Number 22" was emblazoned on the tail in red. Akers and his partner in the aircraft, Mac Mendoza, "were airplane nuts," Akers said. "We were old friends, and we decided we wanted to go air racing. So we figured what's the best airplane for it, and we decided on the Corsair. We just ran it stock." Akers qualified the Corsair in the 10th position at an average speed of 316.67 mph.

The second Corsair at Reno 1967 was owned and flown by Bob

Race Number 11 arrived for the 1968 running of the Reno National Championship Air Races, but the plane is a mystery of sorts. The aircraft, FG-1D N7225C, BuNo 92508, was registered to H.A. Matteri of Santa Rosa, California, and is not listed as an entrant in either the cross-country or pylon races. In addition, John Church raced his Bearcat wearing Race Number 11 in 1967, and Howie Keefe's Mustang received the number in 1969. (Gerry Liang)

Mitchem, who had previously raced AT-6s. As Mitchem arrived from Broomfield, Colorado, in his Goodyear-built FG-1D (BuNo 92050, N194G, Race Number 94) his engine threw two jugs. Mitchem deadsticked the heavily smoking Corsair onto the Stead runway, blowing a tire in the process. The aircraft was stock with minor airframe clean-up having been accomplished. It was bare metal overall, with silver control surfaces and the racing number, 94, in red. Mitchem and his crew attempted an engine change, but were unable to complete the work before the qualifying deadline.

Mitchem's failure to qualify left Akers as the only Corsair in competition. Akers' 10th place qualification put him directly into the Unlimited Consolation Race, as no heat races were run in the Unlimited Class in 1967. The field for the Unlimited Consolation Race consisted of two Mustangs, two Bearcats, one Sea Fury, and Akers' F4U-4. Tom Taylor won the race in Sea Fury N260X, Race Number 33, at an average speed of 336.75 mph. Jim Fugate pulled out of the race during the last lap, and Mike Loening in the P-51D Race Number 2 *Traveler* crossed the finish line fourth, but was dropped to sixth place because he was a fill-in aircraft. Akers finished out of the money in fourth position at 300.78 mph—not a bad finish for a rookie race driver. Mitchem took his racer home and did not return for three years.

Akers returned for the 1968 season at Reno with Race Number 22 fully painted in an overall green with red and gold accents. A pair of jousting lances with trailing ribbons adorned the fuselage, and a knight's shield covered each side of the cowling. The Race Number had been changed from red to gold, and the name *Lancer Two* was painted

The second Corsair to arrive at Reno 1967 made a spectacular entrance. Robert Mitchem of Broomfield, Colorado, was approaching Stead Field when the R-2800 in his FG-1D went south. N194G, BuNo 92050, was smoking heavily when Mitchem deadsticked the fighter onto the runway. As the aircraft touched down, a tire blew. Mitchem safely rolled to a stop, but was unable to repair the plane in time to compete. (Emil Strasser via Gerry Liang)

In 1968, Akers was back, this time with his paint scheme finished. The aircraft wore an overall green Knights of the Round Table scheme with red and gold accents. Two jousting poles adorned the fuselage, a shield was displayed on each side of the cowling, and the aircraft was named Lancer Two. *Akers arrived too late to qualify, but was allowed to compete in order to round out the field of racers. He did not start his first heat race due to a gear malfunction, but did place third in the Unlimited Consolation Race the following day, September 21. (Emil Strasser via Gerry Liang)*

between the jousting lances. "We got a sponsor for the paint job, and it was supposed to be more of a metallic blue than a green," Akers said. "So we took what we got—it was free. I've always been a white knight type, and that's why we had the knight's helmet on the cowling. It was supposed to have been *Lancer's Two* for the two of us—the mechanic and the pilot, but they put *Lancer Two*. They dropped the apostrophe 's' off for some reason. I guess they thought we made a mistake on the sketch for the paint scheme."

Although *Lancer Two* looked fantastic, Akers had arrived too late to qualify. Fortunately, he was allowed to round out the field and compete if he started in the 12th position. During the second Unlim-

ited Class heat race on Friday, September 21, Akers was in the air for the start, but did not enter the racecourse because his gear failed to fully retract. The following day, Akers was moved into the Unlimited Consolation Race's field, where he competed against three P-51Ds, a Bearcat flown by Bob Kucera, and, for the first time in Unlimited air racing, the A-26 Invader (N3328G, Race Number 76) owned and flown by John Lear. The Unlimited pilots elected to allow Lear to race even though his aircraft exceed the 21,000-pound maximum weight limit for Unlimited air racers. When the checkered flag dropped on the Unlimited Consolation Race, John Lear had passed the P-51D flown by Tom Kuchinsky (N6518D, Race

Number 18, *Gen Split Special*), and finished in fifth place with an average speed of 283.68 mph. Dick Kestle finished fourth at 288.43 mph in his P-51D *Miss Diet Rite Cola* (Race Number 13, N6303T) with Akers in *Lancer Two* in third at 301.54 mph. Jim Fugate (P-51D N5077K, Race Number 77) placed second at 306.43 mph behind front place finisher Bob Kucera and his F8F-2 (N212KA, Race Number 99) at 331.85 mph.

In 1969, *Lancer Two* was entered in both the pylon competition and the Harold's Club Transcontinental Trophy Dash from Milwaukee, Wisconsin, to Reno. Six Mustangs, a pair of Bearcats, the *Lancer Two* Corsair, and a Beech Bonanza flown by Judy Wagner made up the racing field for the transcontinental dash. Dick Kestle flew the distance in five hours, 19.3 minutes to win first place. Richard Thomas flew the Corsair in the cross-country race, covering the distance in seven hours, 39.1 minutes to finish in ninth place. Thomas and Wagner, who finished 10th, were actually disqualified because they finished after the 4 P.M. race deadline.

In pylon competition, Akers qualified in 12th position at an average speed of 281.25 mph, quite a bit

slower than his 1967 qualifying speed. To illustrate the speed difference from first to 12th, Darryl Greenamyer in the heavily modified F8F-2 *Conquest I* set a new qualifying speed record of 414.63 mph. Coincidentally, Greenamyer's qualifying speed broke Cook Cleland's 1949 closed course speed record of 397.07 mph, set in the F2G Corsair. Akers placed sixth in the second Unlimited Heat race, turning 296.11 mph, and failed to advance into the money races.

THE DECADE OF THE 1970S AND INTO THE EARLY 1980S

Venues for 1970 included Reno, September 13–20, and the California 1,000-mile pylon race at Mojave, California, held November 13–15. *Lancer Two* missed Reno, but the fans in the stands were treated to the return of Bob Mitchem in Race Number 94 *Big Hummer*. Mitchem had spent the past three seasons modifying the Goodyear-built Corsair. *Big Hummer* qualified in seventh position at an average speed of 362.99, less than 17 mph off that of first place qualifier Clay Lacy's P-51D *Miss Van Nuys* (Race Number 64, N64CL), who turned the pylons at 380.12 mph. Mitchem had replaced the stock engine with a 2,500-horsepower Pratt & Whitney CB-17 from a Douglas DC-6B, which uses a downdraft carburetor. To accommodate the downdraft carburetor, an air scoop was installed over the top of the cowling. A Skyraider prop turned behind a P-51H model spinner, and the cowl flaps were sealed to reduce drag. The stock R-2800 oil cooler was replaced with a unit from an R-4360, and the engine was cooled using a water spraybar system that was fed from a 100-gallon tank located behind the pilot's seat. All of the fabric control sur-

Bob Mitchem returned to race at Reno 1970 after having spent the previous three years modifying his Corsair. The most visible modification was the air scoop over the top of the cowling, feeding the downdraft carburetor of a Pratt & Whitney CB-17 engine from a Douglas DC-6B. Mitchem qualified at 362.99 mph and finished third in the Unlimited Consolation Race at a speed of 357.95 mph. (William T. Larkins)

faces, as well as the wings, were metalized, and the wing retraction mechanism was also removed to lighten the aircraft. In addition, three feet, eight inches was removed from the tips of each wing.

Mitchem flew to a fourth place finish in the first heat race of the weekend, clocking an average speed of 344.40. He placed behind Lyle Shelton's *Able Cat*, which won the race at 369.27 mph, followed by Clay Lacy (357.62 mph), and Howie Keefe at 356.85 mph in the P-51D *Miss America*. Mitchem and *Big Hummer* moved up to the Unlimited Consolation Race, where the Corsair turned in a respectable third place finish at 357.95 mph, finishing only seven seconds behind the winner, Sherman Cooper in the Sea Fury *Miss Merced* (N878M, Race Number 87),

At Mojave in November, Akers was on hand for the 1,000-mile race

After the 1970 Reno races, Gene Akers used the off-season until 1971 to paint his Vought-built Corsair into a more traditional U.S. Navy scheme. At the U.S. Cup Race at Brown Field, near San Diego, California, in July 1972, Akers finished sixth overall. (Gerry Liang)

Bob Guilford's ex-French Aeronavale F4U-7, N33693, BuNo 133693, was also at Brown Field for the U.S. Cup Race. Bob Laidlaw flew Blue Max, *but did not complete the race.* (Gerry Liang)

and so was Bob Guilford in an F4U-7 N693M, BuNo 133693, Race Number 3, *Blue Max. Lancer Two* was now wearing a more military, overall sea blue paint scheme. "The race was real strenuous to fly, especially the time in the 1,000-mile race," Akers said. "It was a three-hour race, and it really took everything out of you. You had to land once and we changed pilots for the remainder of the race. Capt. Carl Birdwell, commanding officer of China Lake's VX-5, took over in the middle of the race." Although Sherman Cooper

won the race at an average speed of 325.92 mph, *Lancer Two* was able to finish 14th, having completed 55 laps followed by *Blue Max* in 16th place, having completed 47 laps.

The following year, 1972, saw four Unlimited Class races: Cape May, New Jersey, June 6; the United States Cup, a 1,000-mile race at Brown Field, San Diego, July 18; Reno's National Championship Air Races, September 12–17; and the California 1,000 at Mojave, California, on November 13. The Cape May race called for the racers to fly 10

laps of a 7.5-mile closed course. Six Mustangs, a pair of Bearcats, one Sea Fury, and the FG-1D owned by John Van Andel made up the Unlimited Field. Ron Reynolds was selected to fly Van Andel's FG-1D in the races. "In late 1970, John Van Andel and I were both supervisors on the 707 at TWA," Reynolds said. "We were always great friends and let each other fly our airplanes; he had a Waco UPF-7 and I had a Staggerwing Beech. I went with John to buy the Corsair out in the San Fernando Valley from David Slica. John was an ex-Navy seaplane and transport pilot, and he bought an FG-1D (N92509, BuNo 92509), which has a rag wing as well as fabric control surfaces. He asked me to fly the Corsair at the Cape May races. Being ex-Air Force, I did not have much time in the Corsair, so I flew it down to Cape May and gingerly around the pylons." Cape May was to be N92509's only race.

On Saturday of the race weekend, the Unlimiteds were in the air ready to start the first heat race. Among the competitors was Shelton in his Bearcat and Ormond Hayden-Bailey in his Sea Fury. "I was starting in the number four position and I said to Bob Hoover as we were starting the race, that I was really

Mitchem returned to Reno in 1971 and during qualifying cut a couple of pylons. He was unable to requalify, and was sidelined for the duration of the races. (Emil Strasser via Gerry Liang)

RACEPLANE**TECH**
S E R I E S

concerned about the fabric control surfaces. I had a real fixation on the ailerons, not knowing when they had last been recovered," Reynolds said. "I asked Hoover if he could start the race a bit slower than he normally would. He brought us down the chute and the last time I looked we were going over 400 mph, which, back then, was pretty fast. We were at full takeoff power, going down hill, and that Corsair was just whistling like hell.

"The Corsair would out-turn a P-51 and certainly a modified Bearcat like Shelton's and certainly a Sea Fury. This was the only race I ever led, even if it was only for 20 seconds or so. We started down into the first turn and I wrapped that Corsair into a pretty good bank. The other guys were going so fast, they went shooting out past me by at least a quarter-mile. All of the sudden I'm on the inside, ahead of the pack. I knew that was not going to last because they all had faster airplanes than I did," Reynolds explained. "I racked the fighter into a bank and held it around the first and second pylon and everyone else was behind me.

"Then I tried to roll out of the turn, and it just stayed there. I looked out on the wing and most of the aileron was gone. I pulled the nose up and was able to exert enough right rudder, with both feet on the right pedal while hauling the stick with both hands to get the wings back to level. As I'm doing this I'm pulling up on the inside of the course. While this is happening, I'm declaring a 'mayday,' and Hoover is coming up onto my wing. But the slower I flew the airplane, the more control I had. I remember that I had the canopy back and was thinking that I had to get out of the airplane. All of a sudden, for whatever reason I don't know, I calmed

Blue Max *competed at Mojave 1974 with Bob Guilford at the controls. He placed seventh in the Unlimited Consolation Race, and ninth in the Championship. (Emil Strasser via Gerry Liang)*

down for a couple of seconds and realized that the aircraft was flying, and I was still going 170 mph, but in a constant left bank. I couldn't totally get the wings level, but at that point I decided to land on one of the cross runways. The chore that I had was to keep it in a bank while timing the altitude so that when I was low enough, the runway was underneath me. For whatever reason, it

worked. I was afraid to put the flaps down for fear of what it would do for the controllability, so I rolled almost wings level, I touched down on the left gear, chopped the power, and after rolling out, taxied back to the ramp."

While Reynolds recovered his composure and thought about the morning's aviation emergency, Van Andel had gone out and found a

Competition on the ramp at Mojave 1974; Blue Max *sits between the P-51D* Candy Man *and the racing P-38 owned by Gary Levitz. (Nicholas A. Veronico Collection)*

Mojave's races were flown in a clockwise fashion, rather than the counterclockwise competition at Reno. In 1975 Bob Guilford turned an average speed of 260.90 mph, ninth place, in the Unlimited Consolation Race. (Emil Strasser via Gerry Liang)

new aileron. Van Andel wanted to continue racing—not from the pilot's seat of course, but Reynolds was still leery of the integrity of the Corsair's fabric covered surfaces. Reynolds relates, "I said, 'John, you know if there is anybody in this world I'd do that for, it is you. But I just don't feel like I'm in the frame of mind to do that.'" Reynolds' narrow escape was the end of N92509's racing career, for Van Andel retired her from the sport and eventually sold the aircraft to the Kalamazoo Aviation History Museum in Kalamazoo, Michigan. Reynolds went on to own a pair of Bearcats, one of which he raced.

In 1978, the Air Museum-Planes of Fame brought F4U-1A N83872, BuNo 17799, to the Reno races. Flown by Jim Maloney, the aircraft qualified at 314.97 mph—not bad for a completely stock Corsair. (Emil Strasser via Gerry Liang)

Both Akers and Guilford showed up for the United States Cup at Brown Field outside of San Diego, California. Fourteen aircraft were to fly 100 laps of a 10-mile closed-course circuit. Bob Laidlaw was slated to fly Guilford's F4U-7 (now renumbered race 93). As it happened at the California 1,000 the previous year, Sherman Cooper again took the checkered flag, flying at an average speed of 330.1 mph. Laidlaw did not finish the race, while Akers turned in a sixth place finish at an average speed of 276 mph.

When September arrived, Guilford and Mitchem headed for the Nevada high country and Stead Field. Gunther Balz in the highly modified P-51D *Roto-Finish Special* and Lyle Shelton in his F8F-2 *Phoenix I* set new Reno qualifying speed records—Balz 419.5 mph and Shelton 418.01 mph. Of the 18 aircraft (nine P-51Ds, three F8Fs, two Sea Furies, two Corsairs, one P-38L, and one P-63) that qualified for the 1971 National Championship Air Races, the Corsairs earned the 16th and 17th positions. Although Mitchem posted a speed of 342.19 mph, he was guilty of cutting a pylon or two and was forced to requalify. Time ran out before he could complete the task, and Mitchem and *Big Hummer* were sidelined for the races. Guilford and *Blue Max* posted a qualifying speed of 289.66 mph. In the Unlimited Medallion Race, new for 1971, Guilford finished the race in sixth place, but was moved into second because four of the racers that finished ahead of him were "fill-in" aircraft. So, in spite of his slow speed, Guilford finished in the money.

The final race of the season was held at Mojave, and both Akers and Guilford showed up to compete. To hold the crowd's interest, the race was changed to 66 laps of a 15.5-mile

The Chino Kids Corsair returned in 1979 for its final racing outing. Maloney qualified the aircraft in 25th position at 319.64 mph. It might have been a fun aircraft to run, but it was not competitive. The group that made up the Chino Kids would return with a more powerful Corsair in 1982. (Emil Strasser via Gerry Liang)

course. The late Frank Sanders was first to finish the race in his Sea Fury at an average speed of 346.55 mph. Akers did exceptionally well and finished fifth with a speed of 314.97 mph. Around the pylons, the Corsair flew "great," Akers said. "With that big, long nose you didn't have to watch the ground at all. You just put the nose a couple of inches below the horizon, and it acted like a big old broomstick coming around the pylons. The nose didn't drop off or come up high like some planes do. It was just an ideal racer, I thought. The Corsair just didn't have enough power." Guilford finished 10th, after completing only 32 laps at an average speed of 264.16 mph.

In 1972, the only racing venue was Reno. Sixteen Unlimited arrived to turn the pylons, and the only Corsair to race was Bob Mitchem's *Big Hummer*. Mitchem posted a 367.50 qualifying speed, and went on to finish fourth in the first Unlimited heat race, turning in an average speed of 363.09 mph. Mitchem flew in the Unlimited Championship Race and turned in a fifth place finish at 341.99 mph. Gunther Balz, in

the highly modified P-51D *Roto-Finish Special*, won the race and set a new Reno and world record speed of 416.16 mph.

At the end of the 1972 season, Gene Akers and his partner sold their Corsair. Like the postwar era Cleveland racers before them, they realized that to be competitive at speeds in excess of 420 mph, they needed to mate an R-4360 to the front end of their Corsair. Without the funds to

devote to modifying the Corsair, Gene Akers retired from air racing. Bob Mitchem retired, too, and his Corsair was sold to another Colorado resident, James Axtell, who planned to get checked out in the Corsair and bring the aircraft west to Reno for the races. Shortly after buying the plane, Axtell's job took him outside the United States. Thus, in the year 2002, Axtell has yet to fly the modified Corsair. It is currently on display at the Wings Over The Rockies Air Museum in Denver. Axtell says he hopes to begin restoration on the Corsair soon. Additionally, astronaut Alan Shepard flew the aircraft during its military history. Unfortunately, someone stole the Corsair's logbooks, and Axtell is currently searching for them.

With Akers and Mitchem out of the competition, only Guilford was left to turn the pylons in a bent-wing bird. His was the sole Corsair on the circuit, consistently turning speeds around 305 mph. Another Corsair finally joined Guilford at Reno in 1978. From the Air Museum–Planes of Fame in Chino, California, came an early F4U-1 (N83782, BuNo 17789, *The Chino Kids*, Race Number

Rookie racer Bob Yancey from Klamath Falls, Oregon, arrived at Reno 1981 with F4U-4 N49092, BuNo 97280, and qualified 19th at 334.93, and flew to a third place finish in the Bronze at 325.765. Yancey would prove to be a tough competitor in the years to come. (Larry Smigla)

0). The late Jim Maloney, who piloted it, qualified at 314.968 mph and finished in the heat race at 282.0 mph. Unfortunately, Maloney's heat race speed was too slow to move up into the money races.

Racing pilot Don Whittington spearheaded a new racing venue for 1979. The Homestead Air Races were held in March 1979 at the airport of the same name, south of Miami, Florida. Twenty-eight racers arrived to compete for $120,000 in prize money. New to the racing circuit were Howard Pardue's ex-Salvadorean Air Force FG-1D (N67HP, BuNo 92095, Fuerza Aerea Sal-

vadorena 211) and Dennis Bradley in the Canadian Warplane Heritage's FG-1D (C-GCWX, BuNo 92436). Speeds in Miami were rather low, with Bill Whittington winning the stock class race in his P-63 at a speed of 287.769 mph. Bradley finished sixth (278.822 mph) with Pardue coming in seventh (250.447 mph).

Jim Maloney and Bob Guilford were back for the 1979 Reno races. Out of a field of 28 racers, Guilford qualified 22nd (330.70 mph) followed by Maloney, 25th at 319.64 mph. Guilford placed sixth in the Bronze race (252.124 mph), and Maloney did not move up. Although Jim Maloney

and his brother John would be back to race in future years, Reno '79 was the last racing outing for the Planes of Fame Corsair. Guilford's *Blue Max* was the only Corsair to race at Reno the following year. Twenty-two aircraft arrived to race in the Unlimited Class, and Guilford qualified in the 21st position at 312.95 mph. Blue Max competed in the Bronze race, finishing sixth at an average speed of 285.11 mph.

A new Corsair arrived on the Reno ramp in 1981. *Blue Max* was there to race, as was rookie Robert Yancey's F4U-4 (N49092, BuNo 97280, Race Number 101). Yancey's

Steve Hinton said they started the Super Corsair *project with a hulk, and he meant it. This is the F4U fuselage that later became the Super Corsair. During the spring and early summer of 1982, an all-volunteer crew transformed this hulk by mating an R-4360 to the fuselage, and four races later it won the Unlimited Gold Race at Reno 1985.* (Nicholas A. Veronico)

By Reno 1983, most of the bugs were being worked out of the Super Corsair, *and the racer was turning speeds on average of 405 mph. Hinton flew the R-4360-powered* Bud Light Special *to a first-place finish in the 1983 Unlimited Silver Race. He ran the Race at an average 417.097 mph.* (Gerry Liang)

Corsair was one of eight recovered from Honduras during 1978 and 1979 by Jim Nettle's Hollywood Wings, which was financially backed by Howard Pardue and Bob Ferguson. Six of the eight Corsairs were flown from Honduras to Texas, where they were put up for sale. Yancey's aircraft had flown for the Fuerza Aerea Hondurena as FAH-615. Yancey qualified at 334.93 mph (19th), impressive for the rookie, followed by Guilford at 323.67 mph (22nd out of 25). Both Corsairs competed in the Bronze race, Yancey finishing third (325.765 mph) with Guilford finishing a distant fourth at 247.779 mph.

RETURN OF THE
R-4360-POWERED CORSAIR

Not since the Cleveland days of Cook Cleland, Dick Becker, Ben McKillen, and Ron Puckett had an R-4360-powered Corsair turned the pylons. But that all changed when the racers arrived at Reno for 1982 National Championship Air Races. The modified Mustangs, Bearcats, and Sea Furies now faced a new, highly modified R-4360-powered Corsair owned by the Air Museum-Planes of Fame and flown by Jim Maloney and Steve Hinton. The R-4360-powered Corsair was an immediate hit with the Reno racing enthusiasts.

Hinton's business, Fighter Rebuilders, is colocated at the museum, and it was here that a stock F4U-1A Corsair hulk was transformed into the R-4360-powered *Super Corsair*. "Jim Maloney and I went to the opening of Doug Champlin's fighter museum in Mesa, Arizona, in late 1981," Hinton said. "One of the aircraft in Doug's collection was an F2G Corsair. We were crawling around, looking at it, and joking about flying it, and that's what sparked the thought originally. As soon as we got home from the weekend, we called Bruce Boland and asked him what he thought of the F2G Corsair. Engine builder Dave Zueschel would laugh. He thought it would do pretty good, but there was no way it could stay with the Mustangs. I asked Bruce, and he too laughed at the idea. About a week later, Bruce called back and said he was playing around with the airspeed/horsepower curves on that Corsair and believed it would be pretty fast. Our friend John Sandberg happened to be in the office when Bruce called back and offered an R-4360 to the project.

The sun glints off the fuselage of Race Number 101 as the late afternoon Nevada skies darken. Yancey flew the Corsair to a second-place finish in the 1982 Bronze, at an average speed of 355.530 mph. (Chuck Aro)

"Bruce did the engineering, John Paul gave us a set of wings, and here at Fighter Rebuilders we were between a couple of deadlines during the summer of 1982, so we decided to give it a big effort and do all we could do to get it to Reno in September. We went from a bare fuselage to a flying airplane from May to August. It was a real all-out effort, 10 hours a day, seven days a week," Hinton related. "Once we started on it we had friends that came by to offer their help. George Byard from Aircraft Cylinder pitched in with another R-4360 that we could scavenge for the QEC parts we needed. Brian Cole of Con-

Yancey's Race Number 101 Corsair taxies past the Reno home pylon during the 1982 races. (Gerry Liang)

FG-1D N4715C, BuNo 67089, Race Number 82, was the third of four Corsairs to arrive at Reno for the 1982 races. Flown by Mike Wright, the basically stock bent-wing finished fifth in the Unlimited Bronze class at 275.610 mph. (Gerry Liang)

The aircraft attracting the most attention was the fourth Corsair on the 1982 Reno ramp—the Bud Light Super Corsair, *Race Number 1. Built up from an F4U fuselage, this aircraft was the first R-4360-powered Corsair to turn the pylons since the 1949 Cleveland National Air Races 33 years earlier. (Emil Strasser via Gerry Liang)*

solidated Aeronautics was generous with parts; Wally McDonnell had some Corsair parts we traded for; Frank Sanders was a big help to us too, but his biggest help was that he jokingly told us we couldn't do it. The same with Lloyd Hamilton. He said, 'You're wasting your time, that thing will never go fast.' As we were getting closer, they both became very supportive too. Dennis Sanders helped us on the project very much. A lot of companies and individuals kicked in money, parts, and pieces, and made this racer possible.

"When we were designing the engine mount, the fuselage was a totally hollow, empty shell. It didn't even have landing gear, so we sat it low to the ground on wing jacks to zero out the thrust line to get the prop shaft exactly perfect. We put the prop shaft right where it was when the aircraft had an R-2800 installed, and it was actually only one inch longer than a stock F4U-1, because we put the 4360 right up against the firewall. We used a C-97 engine ring, cut all the C-97 legs off it, and Boland designed a mount with the proper tubing. Randy Scoville fabricated the bathtub fittings, and we bolted them on the airframe. That was quite an experience." The engine cowling began life as an A-26 speed ring, which Hinton and

Bob Guilford's Race 93 and Bob Yancey's Race 101 on the pit ramp. Five Corsairs of various models arrived to race at Reno 1984. Hinton, Yancey, Guilford, and Wright were joined by J.K. Ridley's Race Number 37 Big Richard, *and F4U-4, N4908M, BuNo 96995. (Gerry Liang)*

Boland happened onto while walking through the museum brainstorming about the project. Having access to the museum's collection allowed the team to walk through and see how different aircraft manufacturers solved certain problems.

When the aircraft's systems were being installed, the fuel tank was located forward of the cockpit, as in stock Corsairs. Water tanks were installed in each wing to feed the oil cooler spraybars and the engine spraybar, which was fitted inside the cowling speed ring. The oil cooler inlet ducts were closed down and coolers from a Grumman S2F were fitted. To accommodate the R-4360's P.R. 100 downdraft carburetor, the speed ring from an A-26 was installed and the remainder of the cowling built up. A 35-gallon oil tank and a 25-gallon ADI tank were located behind the pilot's seat. The wings were clipped 3 1/2 feet, and Boland-designed tips were fabricated from fiberglass. The outer flap was deleted, and faired into the wing.

"Once we got the thing flying, Frank Sanders could not stay with us in a stock Sea Fury when we were just flying around the airport. That's what sparked him into building the R-4360-powered *Dreadnought*," Hinton said. "I remember the first time we turned on the water injection on in the Corsair and Frank was flying chase. From our little practice area back to the airport is only about 11 or 12 miles, and by the time the Corsair got back over the airport at Chino, Jim Maloney was flying it at that time, he had about a five-mile jump on the Sea Fury. Frank was absolutely flabbergasted.

"We had a lot of problems with the *Super Corsair* after we got it flying. Getting it in the air was the big issue, and then refining it was a never-ending job. It took us two years to get the flight controls to be

Underside view gives a good idea to how short the Super Corsair's *wings were. The aircraft's wingspan was reduced seven feet from its factory delivered 41-foot span.* (Gerry Liang)

The freshly built instrument panel of the Super Corsair. (Jim Dunn)

acceptable. The ailerons are made of wood and they are designed with 300-mph normal speeds, so when you are up around 400 mph, they are really touchy. They are a freeze design—where the leading edge actually goes into the wind, so to speak, to boost the trailing edge going into the wind. So it's a balancing-type of aileron. At those speeds, the leading edge actually does more balancing than the trailing edge, so that was a problem we encountered the first couple of years with those ailerons. You get over 440 mph, and boy, sometimes the stick would just do what it wants to—and you just kinda hang on. It was scary the first time we encountered it—it's just a terrible feeling. We were coming up with these strips of aluminum on the wing to try to change the profile, just Band-Aids here and there. Then we finally built a set of ailerons with just a little different shape than the original, and that took care of the problem.

"Also, directional stability was marginal on a Corsair anyway, and then we put all of that extra propeller and horsepower on it and it took quite a bit of development to work through that too. We ended up metalizing the control surfaces because we blew the fabric off them a couple of times. It would easily indicate above 400 mph, which was about all the fabric surfaces are good for on a horizontal surface. They weren't meant to do that regularly. It would do it in a dive or in a combat situation, but not on a daily basis.

"We ran pretty much stock horsepower, 3,800 horsepower, but a couple of times we ran it up over 4,000. Part of our deal was that we wanted to win, but we didn't want to blow it up. The first engine we had was a stock engine, an R-4360–63 out of a Globemaster. We

The Super Corsair's exhaust tubing was custom designed and fabricated at Chino during the racer's 5-month transformation. (Chuck Aro)

Steve Hinton discusses the aircraft's potential with a crew from ABC's Wide World of Sports on the Reno ramp shortly after the Super Corsair *arrived for the 1982 races. Hinton's previous Unlimited class wins included Reno 1978 and Mojave 1978 and 1979 while flying the Griffon-powered P-51* Red Baron. *(Gerry Liang)*

made no changes to it other than adding a prop shaft nose case from a –59 which had a 60-spline shaft so we could fit a Skyraider prop on it. We changed the accessory drive to a position that didn't hit the engine mount and that kind of stuff. We ran that engine for the first four years at Reno (1982–1985).

"It was a great project, a lot of people involved with it, and thousands and thousands of hours of work. It taxes your brain and all of your resources, but that was something we wanted to do at that time, and that's why we did it."

CORSAIR COMPETITION

At Reno 1982, Yancey had named his Corsair *Old Blue* and qualified at 346.86 mph. Guilford was back, too, and he posted a speed of 333.43 mph. A Corsair new to the racing circuit was Mike Wright's Race FG-1D No. 82 (N4715C, BuNo 67089) *Wart Hog,* which qualified at 304.4 mph. Although Wright did not make the 21-aircraft racing field, he was allowed to race as the first alternate after Dan Martin's *Ridge Runner* blew an engine and was forced to belly land in the sagebrush. All three of the stock Corsairs competed in the Unlimited Bronze race, Yancey finishing second (355.53 mph), followed by Guilford in fourth (308.375 mph), and Wright in fifth (275.610 mph). Three Corsairs in one heat—it just doesn't get any better.

The Unlimited Gold Race was run on Sunday, September 19, with a field of six P-51Ds, including the heavily modified *Dago Red* and *Sumthin' Else,* and Hinton in the *Super Corsair.* The eight-lap race around the 9.187-mile course was over in less than 10 minutes, and after penalties were assessed for pylon cuts, Hinton had finished in fourth place at an average speed of

Mike Wright made flying the Corsair look fun. He always flew a low, tight course, as demonstrated by this turn passing Pylon 8. (Gerry Liang)

362.50 mph. A precursor of what was to come from the *Super Corsair.*

Mike Wright did not return for 1983, but the previous year's trio of Corsairs did show for Reno's 20th National Championship Air Races. Hinton posted a 408.31-mph qualifying speed in the *Super Corsair's* second outing. Yancey turned in a respectable 370.82-mph run, followed by Guilford at 316.67 mph. Guilford's speeds that year were too slow to move up to the money races. Yancey competed in the Bronze race against John Maloney in the P-51D, Race Number 0 *Spam Can.* Maloney would later move into the cockpit of the *Super Corsair.* Yancey flew to a third place finish at 362.651 mph.

A second racing venue, in addition to Reno, was added for the 1984 season. Moose Jaw, Saskatchewan, Canada, held races in June. Eight Mustangs, a pair of Sea Furies, and the Corsairs of Mike Wright and Bob Yancey arrived to compete for the

prize money. Both Corsairs competed in the Unlimited Silver Race, Wright pulling out before the start of the race with landing gear troubles, and Yancey taking third at 324.416 mph.

Reno 1984 saw the largest gathering of racing Corsairs since the Cleveland days. Thirty-one aircraft arrived to compete, including five Corsairs, with Neil Anderson in *Dreadnought* posting the top qualifying speed of 442.747 mph. Hinton, Yancy, Guilford, and Wright were joined by rookie J.K. "Buck" Ridley and his F4U-4, Race Number 37 *Big Richard* (N4908M, BuNo 96995). Hinton qualified at 424.015 mph, and took third in the Unlimited Gold Race, finishing behind the highly modified Mustangs *Stiletto* and *Sumthin' Else.* In the Silver race, Yancey declared a mayday before the start, and landed safely, but he was out of the competition for the year. The three slower Corsairs competed in the nine-plane Unlimited

It was "run what ya brung" at Reno 1985 when Mike Wright switched racing mounts from the Corsair *Wart Hog* to the A-26 *Puss & Boots*. Wright qualified the twin R-2800 racer at 301.482 mph, and battled Fred Sebby in the Unlimited Bronze Race. (Nicholas A. Veronico)

Bronze race, in which Mustangs placed one, two, and three, followed by Buck Ridley in fourth (320.922 mph). Wright and Guilford only completed five laps before the race was declared over.

Bakersfield, California, hosted an Unlimited class race on May 30, 1985. Everyone thought its proximity, 150 miles north of Los Angeles and 200 miles south of San Francisco, would guarantee its success. Twelve Unlimiteds arrived to race, including five Mustangs, four Sea Furies, a pair of Bearcats, and the *Super Corsair*. Ron Hevle flew the modified P-51 *Dago Red* to a first place finish at 431.451 mph, followed by Lyle Shelton in *Rare Bear* at 418.774 mph, with Steve Hinton following third at 412.999 mph. Although the fans enjoyed the venue, it was unable to meet its financial needs and the race was not repeated.

Reno 1985 was once again a five-Corsair race. Out of the 32 qualifiers, Hinton posted the fifth highest speed at 431.944 mph. Yancey turned in a 368.062-mph run, while Ridley and Guilford posted 338.767 mph and 326.732 mph respectively. The newcomer was Alan Preston in an F4U-5NL night fighter, *Old Deadeye* (Race Number 12, BuNo 124559, N4901W), who qualified at 332.891 mph. Wiley Sanders in his P-51D, *Jeannie Too*, won the Bronze race at a speed of 355.725 mph. In fifth place was Ridley (320.922 mph), followed by Preston at 314.878 mph. In the Silver, the always competitive Yancey led the race from the start until the final few feet, when Tom Kelley in the P-51D *Lou IV* traded altitude for speed and dove past Yancey to win the race. Kelley's final average speed was 374.418 mph versus Yancey's 374.392 mph. One of the closest races on record.

The Unlimited Gold Race saw the R-4360-powered *Super Corsair* and Sea Furies *Dreadnought*, flown by Neil Anderson, and *Furias*, flown by Lloyd Hamilton, go head-to-head with the Mustangs of Rick Brickert (*Dago Red*), Bud Granley (*Miss America*), John Crocker (*Sumthin' Else*), Skip Hom (*Stiletto*), and Ron Hevle (*Strega*). The classic Merlin versus

Heat Race 1 at Reno 1984 featured the three Corsairs of J.K. Ridley, Guilford, and Yancey, who finished the race first. Yancey's Corsair, *Old Blue*, flew the six-lap race at an average of 349.033 mph. (Emil Strasser)

R-4360 duel was on. The Mustangs of Hevle and Holm did not start the race—Holm could not retract the gear, and Hevle burned a piston as the racers came down the chute. When the race got under way, Hinton and the *Super Corsair* steadily moved up through the pack. Crocker broke a connecting rod on the back side of lap six, and Granley pulled out of the race on lap seven, when he was mistakenly given the checkered flag instead of the white flag on lap seven. That left Brickert to contend with the three R-4360-powered racers. Hinton was putting pressure on Anderson and it came down to the last lap. "We (the *Super Corsair* team) were flying the plane as best as we could, hoping to get up close to the front of the pack," Hinton said. "With a stroke of luck, the leader cut a pylon on the last lap. We won, which was great, and then we found out it was a course speed record, too!" Anderson had cut the last pylon on the last lap and was penalized, moving Hinton into first place. Brickert finished third at 426.848 mph, followed by Hamilton at 411.952 mph. Hinton's record average race speed, 438.186 mph, would hold for another two years. After this Unlimited Gold Race victory, he moved on to fly the new, custom-built Unlimited racer *Tsunami* at Reno 1986. John Maloney now took over full-time duties at the stick of the *Super Corsair*.

Reno was the sole venue for 1986, and Rick Brickert had moved into the driver's seat of *Dreadnought*. He went out and set a new qualifying record of 452.737 mph. John Maloney posted a qualifying speed of 422.006 mph in the *Super Corsair*. Yancey qualified at 391.085 mph, his fastest speed ever, while Guilford turned in a speed of 325.994 mph. Guilford advanced into the Bronze race, but only finished five laps before the race

Bruce Lockwood examines the blown out canopy of Alan Preston's Old Deadeye. Preston lost the canopy during Unlimited Heat 1C. He went on to place sixth in the Unlimited Bronze at an average speed of 314.878 mph. This was the only Reno outing for Preston's night fighter Corsair, as he moved up to the driver's seat of the modified P-51 Dago Red the following year. (Jim Dunn)

Alan Preston arrived ready to race at Reno 1985 in a night fighter F4U-5NL N4901W, Race Number 12, BuNo 124569. This aircraft was returned from Honduras in 1978 and subsequently restored before being acquired by Preston in 1984. (Gerry Liang)

Blue Max down low. Although Guilford and the F4U-7 were not competitive in the Unlimited Gold Race, the stock Corsair was a pleasure to watch turning the pylons at around 325 mph. At Reno 1985, Blue Max *was one of five bent-wing birds turning the pylons.* (Gerry Liang)

was over. Yancey competed in the Silver, turning in a fifth place finish at 379.772 mph. Maloney took the *Super Corsair* to a sixth place finish in Heat 2B. The *Super Corsair* had a carburetor problem that burned a couple of pistons, putting Maloney and the team out of the running.

On May 10, 1987, Bob Guilford was attending an air show at Brown Field, near San Diego, California. Another pilot and a passenger were in the plane when it crashed, destroying the aircraft and killing both occupants. *Blue Max* was gone. Guilford would return to racing, only later in a Sea Fury.

When the aircraft arrived to race at Reno that year, John Maloney and Bob Yancey flew the two competing Corsairs. Yancey qualified 24th in a field of 25, at an average speed of 308.285 mph. Maloney turned the pylons at 431.607 mph for a sixth-place posting. Bill "Tiger" Destefani set a qualifying record that year of 466.674 mph in the modified P-51D *Strega*. Maloney went on to place fourth in the Unlimited Gold Race, clocking an average speed of 416.905 mph. Yancey sold his Corsair to concentrate on his new, and in comparison to the F4U, radically different Yak-11 racer.

Gary Meermans was the rookie racing Corsair driver at Reno 1988. He qualified at 315.447 mph in his Goodyear-built FG-1D *Sky Boss*, Race Number 111, formerly *Wart Hog*. He failed to make the field. Maloney and his team qualified the *Super Corsair* at 442.319 mph. During Heat Race 1-A, Maloney ran the *Super Corsair* wide open for the entire race, pulling 69 inches of manifold pressure at 2,900 rpms, producing 4,050 horsepower. His average speed for the entire race was 445.072 mph—first place. In Heat 2-A he placed fourth, 420.177 mph, and pulled out of Heat 3-A with a sick engine. Maloney ran the Unlimited Gold Race but was running in sixth place when the race had ended.

By Reno 1989, John Maloney and the *Super Corsair* team were the only bent-wing bird flying the racing circuit. Kevin Eldridge took over *Super Corsair* flying duties in 1992. He'd served as crew chief from 1983 to 1989, and began racing the museum's P-51D *Spam Can* in 1990. "It's a little bit different feel in the Mustang and the Bearcat," Eldridge said. "You feel like part of the airplane. The cockpit is nice and comfortable, where the Corsair was kind of archaic. You sat up higher, and felt like you were sitting on top of it versus being in a small cockpit as one unit with the plane. The *Super Corsair* was an early Corsair with no floorboards, just channels for your feet. If you dropped your chart, it went all the way to the bottom. On the other hand, that made it good for installing the fuel pump and our ADI equipment." Maloney and Eldridge consistently raced the Corsair in the 415- to 430-mph range.

THE END OF AN ERA

When the *Super Corsair* arrived at the Phoenix 500 Air Races in 1994, the airplane's engine was acting up. It was burning a piston here and there, it was not pulling the torque it should, and the team was working to diagnose the problem. Even with a tempestuous engine, Eldridge qualified the racer at 428.104 mph, consistent with what the plane had

been running during its previous races. In Heat 1-A, Eldridge flew to a slow, sixth-place finish at an average speed of 355.440 mph.

On Saturday of race weekend, Eldridge took off for the running of the Unlimited Silver Race and joined up for the air start. Eldridge picks up the story: "The poor deal at Phoenix was that we didn't have a pace plane. Howard Pardue, even though he was racing, was going to be the pace plane. He's like dog and ponying it, going real slow, and then all of the sudden we have a race and he slams the throttle. So I was just pacing him and waiting for my spot to pass, and about the third lap the engine really started running rough. To put it into perspective, it's like running over a bunch of speed bumps in your car.

"So I pulled the power back about 10 inches, and it was still doing it. I was on the front stretch and I declared a mayday and pulled up. I pulled the power off and it was no big deal. I was going to turn down wind and land.

"Then the guys said over the radio that I had smoke, then that I had fire. Next I heard the fire was out. Then it came back. So I hit the fire bottles. I didn't want to go out or anything. Everybody was yelling at me to bail out. Robbie Patterson was flying with Bob Hoover in a TF-51, and Johnny Maloney was on the radio yelling to me that there was a big fire and that I should bail out.

"I probably climbed up to 2,000 feet and I got it back to 250 mph. I pointed the nose off from down-wind about a 45-degree angle out to the desert and just proceeded to get everything unhooked. One of the things we didn't have in the cockpit was an aileron trim. We would set the tab for flying cross-country, and then when we got to the race we would adjust the tab for the high

Above: *Yancey's* Old Blue *is about to pass Howard Pardue's XF8F-1 Bearcat during Unlimited Heat 1B at Reno 1985. Yancey went on to win the race at an average speed of 368.819 mph. The size difference of the two R-2800-powered Navy fighters can be discerned from the fuselage lengths as well as diameters, and a comparison of the aircrafts' wingspan.* (Chuck Aro)

Below: *Steve Hinton flew the* Super Corsair *to a new Unlimited Gold Race speed of 438.186 mph, and captured the first-place finish when Neil Anderson in* Dreadnought *was penalized for cutting a pylon. Hinton's victory was the first for an R-4360-powered Corsair since 1949, and an amazing feat when you consider that less than three years earlier, the plane was a hulk sitting behind The Air Museum-Planes of Fame at Chino.* (Nicholas A. Veronico)

After seeing the R-4360 and Corsair engine-airframe combination in flight, Frank Sanders and sons Brian and Dennis mated an R-4360 to the fuselage of an ex-Burmese Air Force Hawker Sea Fury T.Mk 20. Neil Anderson flew the super Sea Fury in the Unlimited Gold Race at Reno 1985. He was leading the race and crossed the finish line first, but was penalized for cutting pylon 8 on lap 8. (Nicholas A. Veronico)

speeds of racing. It was, of course, set for racing so when I got it back to about 250 mph, it wouldn't fly straight and level. It wanted to roll on me.

"I was getting all unhooked and getting ready to hop out, and I was going to bail out to the left but the Corsair wanted to roll to the right. In the process of jumping on the seat to

Yancey's goal was to increase the performance of his Corsair without making too many radical external changes, and still remain competitive. The most visible change was cutting the canopy down, and after Alan Preston's experience, it seemed the smart thing to do. (Jim Dunn)

stand on the seat to jump overboard, my foot slipped and I got stuck in between the seat and the fuselage. I was stuck—big time!

"I had the canopy open and was pushing with everything I had, and I physically broke my leg to get out of the cockpit—which I didn't know at the time. I was just pushing. So instead of getting a good jump out, I just flopped over the side to the left.

"The last thing I remember is looking at the greasy side of the airplane as I flopped over the side. Then all of the sudden it was wham-bam! What had happened was that when I went over the side, I hit the airstream and flew right into the tail. I hit the horizontal with the top of my head and my right forearm. It broke my neck and my arm. It was so fast I don't really feel anything. Just wham! And the next thing I know I'm spinning in the air and thinking that I've got to pull the D-ring. I'm spinning and I'm feeling for the D-ring, and I can't find it. Finally I looked down at the chute and the tube is there, but there's no D-ring, and I thought 'Well, that's it. I'm gonna go in here.' Then all the sudden the chute popped open. I think that when I hit the tail and started spinning it flung the D-ring out.

"I was hanging in the chute, but I didn't get a chance to see the airplane go down. Robbie and Bob Hoover circled me, and I waved at them. My right arm hurt a little bit and my neck was a little stiff, but I didn't think much about it. Then I looked down, and my left foot was pointed 90 degrees the wrong way! I thought, 'This is gonna hurt!'

"I was floating down, and it seemed like it was in slow motion. Behind me there was this two-lane highway. And there was a white diesel truck coming down the road, and I'm making a beeline for this road. I'm hanging there thinking,

Maloney is one of the first to start for the 1989 Unlimited Gold Race. Six planes of the nine aircraft field can be seen in this view. From left: the Super Corsair, Tsunami, Dreadnought, Strega, *and* Rare Bear. *P-51D* Cottonmouth *is parked at the end of the row.* Strega *was forced out on lap 6 with coolant problems, and Lyle Shelton went on to win the race at 450.910 mph. Rick Brickert followed in* Dreadnought *at 427.871 mph, with Maloney placing third at 406.265 mph. (Nicholas A. Veronico)*

'Now I'm gonna get hit by this truck! I can't win here.' There was just a bit of breeze, so I held my arms out, and it was just enough resistance to help me pass just over the road. Then I held that leg up that was broken, and I hit, kind of rolled, hit the ground there, and was still thinking to myself 'Well, that wasn't too bad … I'll just sit up.' Well that was all I wrote, because I couldn't sit up. I just laid out there, and eventually they came out with a helicopter and they got me."

The *Super Corsair's* engine had split wide open, and Eldridge was lucky to be alive. Reflecting on his association with the *Super Corsair*, Eldridge said, "I loved that airplane; it was a good airplane. We had a great group of guys and everybody pitched in all the time. We just kind of lived and breathed that thing for several years. We were trying to refine it there at the end as far as spraybar systems, so we could have gotten a few more mph out of it. It had such a fat wing and it was probably real close to its limit. One of the last things Bruce Boland had talked to us about was for the airplane to go any faster, we would have to create a new leading edge for the wing—kind of a false leading edge that would bring it out a little bit and make it smaller. That would have been quite a bit of work, but that had been talked about. It was a good consistent 440-450-mph racer."

Since the loss of the *Super Corsair*, a bent-wing bird has not been entered into competition. The value of a stock warbird Corsair has reached prices in excess of $1 million, and there are no unrestored F4U airframes ready to be converted into racing aircraft. It's now up to the R-3350- and R-4360-powered Sea Furies and Bearcats to continue the round-engine versus Merlin debate.

Competition for the Super Corsair *in the 1985 Unlimited Gold Race included* Dago Red, *foreground, flown by Alan Preston, and* Miss America, *piloted by Bud Granley. This uncowled view of* Dago Red *in the pits shows the extent of the modifications required to make a Mustang competitive. (Nicholas A. Veronico)*

At Reno 1986, the Super Corsair's *R-4360 suffered from carburetor problems and burned a couple of pistons. In spite of the team's hard work, the* Super Corsair *was out of competition for the year. Note the propeller spinner afterbody, which the team custom built to improve airflow to the engine.* (Nicholas A. Veronico)

The aircraft almost disappears as the Super Corsair's *R-4360 comes to life in a cloud of smoke.* (Chuck Aro)

Gary Meermans came to race at Reno 1988 in Race 111, formerly Race 82 Wart Hog, but his qualifying speed was too low to make the field. Compare the wing flaps of Meermans' stock FG-1D (below) to those of the Super Corsair (left). The R-4360-powered Corsair's third flap has been faired into the wing, reducing the weight of the aircraft by removing the flap mechanisms, while also increasing its aerodynamic cleanliness by eliminating the flap gaps. (Gerry Liang)

The year following his Unlimited Gold Race victory, Steve Hinton moved on to fly John Sandberg's custom-built, Merlin-powered Tsunami. The aircraft never reached its full racing potential, before it crashed, killing Sandberg, as he ferried the aircraft home from the 1991 Reno races. (Armand H. Veronico)

John Maloney brings the Bud Light-sponsored Corsair in to land after one of the heat races at Reno 1988. Plagued by engine trouble that year, the racer dropped out of Heat Race 3A, and only finished sixth in the Unlimited Gold. (Emil Strasser)

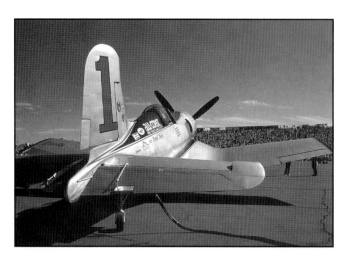

For the Unlimited Gold Race, the aircraft are parked in front of the stands while the pilots are introduced to the crowd. Once the introductions have ended, the racers come to life. The crew disconnects the ground power cart and gives the aircraft one final visual inspection. Then the racers taxi out past the crowd for the air start, Super Corsair leading the TF-51 Lady Jo. The 1993 Unlimited Gold Race was won by Bill "Tiger" Destefani in Strega at an average speed of 455.380 mph. Eldridge finished fifth, flying the course at 418.656 mph. (Nicholas A. Veronico)

RACEPLANE **TECH**
S E R I E S

The Super Corsair *poses for a pre-race team photo at Reno 1989; back row, from left: Daryl Bond, Rob Patterson, John Maloney, Mike McDougall, Kevin Eldridge, Matt Nightingale, and Karen Hinton; front row from left: Annie Butkiewicz, Matt Mauch, Joe Tidwell, John Hinton, Alan Wojciak, Bill Barclay, and Pat Nightingale. (Nicholas A. Veronico)*

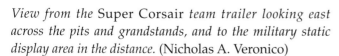

View from the Super Corsair *team trailer looking east across the pits and grandstands, and to the military static display area in the distance. (Nicholas A. Veronico)*

Dangling ignition wires and dripping oil look like a nightmare to most passers-by in the pits, but not to the dedicated crew of the Super Corsair. *(Gerry Liang)*

Steve Hinton, left, and Super Corsair *crew chief Kevin Eldridge celebrate after Hinton's 1985 Unlimited Gold Race win. Appropriately, the crew celebrates with the product of its sponsor, Bud Light. That's the spirit of a winning team.* (Shawn Aro)

Above: *Howard Pardue, left, and John Maloney wait to be introduced to the Reno crowd prior to the 1986 Unlimited Gold Race. This was Maloney's first year as chief pilot of the* Super Corsair. (Nicholas A. Veronico)

The Super Corsair *racing team's crew for 1993 included, from left: Mike McBuckian, Bob Reed, Jerry Wilkins, Kevin Eldridge with young Steve "Stevo" Hinton, Chris Fahey, Matt Nightingale, and John Hinton.* (Nicholas A. Veronico)

Kevin Eldridge taxies toward the runway for what would become the Super Corsair's *final flight at the 1994 Phoenix 500. Less than 10 minutes later the R-4360-powered Corsair was on fire headed for the desert floor, and a badly injured Eldridge was floating back to earth dangling from a parachute. Although the* Super Corsair *was a total loss, Eldridge made a full recovery and went on to race again.* (Chuck Aro)

RACING 4 BEARCATS

THE FASTEST CATS IN THE WORLD

The early 1960s were a different time technologically for the U.S. Navy. No longer did racers have to approach Navy brass for the favor of releasing an aircraft from the inventory. The 1960s U.S. Navy was moving to a pure jet force, its air superiority fighters having made the transition to the Chance Vought F8U Crusader, Grumman F11F Tiger, and the McDonnell F4H (later F-4) Phantom II. While the Navy transitioned from props, the older aircraft were sent to Naval Reserve units and then eventually to its storage facilities. In the mid-1950s, the largest of the Navy's storage sites was the long-term storage facility at Litchfield Park, 20 miles west of Phoenix, Arizona. By March 1958, approximately 2,500 aircraft, primarily of World War II vintage, were sitting in the desert at Litchfield Park awaiting a civilian buyer or the scrapper's torch.

Grumman's propeller-driven fighter line had evolved through the biplanes FF, SF, F2F, and F3F to theF4F Wildcat, F6F Hellcat, and F7F Tigercat of World War II. Its ultimate extension was the F8F Bearcat. Developed too late to see service in World War II, the Bearcat had an empty weight (7,070 pounds) that was nearly a ton lighter than the F6F Hellcat (9,238 pounds) and powered by a more powerful 2,100-horsepower R-2800-34W radial engine. The last of 1,263 F8Fs of all variants was delivered in May 1949, and the Navy began retiring some of its earlier Bearcats in 1952. Pilots with a lust for speed and a bit of disposable income could purchase a surplus F8F from

Litchfield Park, inspect the plane, make any necessary repairs, and have a high-performance fighter as a personal aircraft. Many people did purchase surplus Bearcats from the Navy, and word of Stead's revival of the National Air Races attracted the attention of many aviators.

One of the first pilots to inquire about the upcoming races was Walt Ohlrich Jr. "My interest in air racing started when, as a boy, I watched many of the Cleveland Air Races,"

recalled Ohlrich. "I always had the idea that someday I would like to try it myself." Ohlrich, who was in the Navy at the time, called Bill Stead, got all the information, and immediately went about looking for a fast piston-engine airplane. "During the 1950s, surplus airplanes were in great abundance on every airport in the United States," said Ohlrich. "When I looked around, however, I was shocked to find that most of the World War II aircraft had disap-

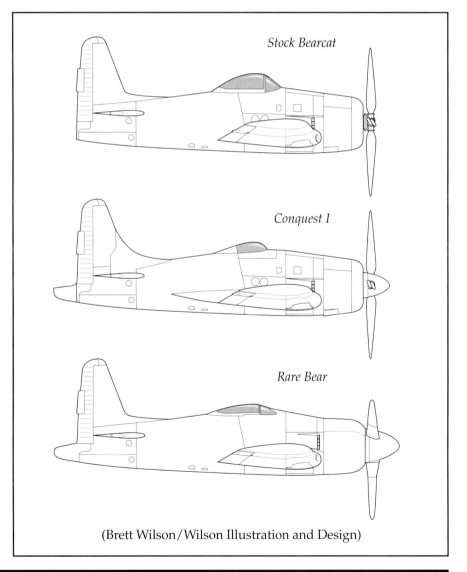

Stock Bearcat

Conquest I

Rare Bear

(Brett Wilson/Wilson Illustration and Design)

Three Grumman F8F-2 Bearcats competed in the first Reno National Championship Air Race. To the extreme right is Darryl Greenamyer's Race Number 1; center is Bill Stead's Bearcat, which was piloted by Mira Slovak, Race Number 80; and in the background is Walt Ohlrich's Race Number 10. (Robert F. Pauley via Tim Weinschenker)

Darryl Greenamyer (left) accepting the National Championship Trophy from Bob Hoover. In 1965 Greenamyer qualified first at 369.70 mph. He placed second in Heat 1 and first in Heat 3, and won the Championship Race at 375.10 mph. (Robert F. Pauley via Tim Weinschenker)

peared. A lead on a Corsair fell through. I almost gave up, when I met Tom Matthews who had recently purchased an F8F-2 that had been sitting in the desert awhile. Tom was having it made ready for license where I was based in Monterey, California. To make a long story short, he asked me to test fly it and later take it to Reno in 1964. Wow!"

Darryl Greenamyer, a newly hired Lockheed test pilot, had pur-

chased a Bearcat in mid-1964 after hearing about the advent of the races. While he waited for his security clearance at Lockheed, Greenamyer went about getting the craft race-ready by reducing the airplane's overall weight. He removed the heavy rubber self-sealing fuel bladder and sealed the compartment between the front and rear wing spars to enable the Bearcat to carry 310 gallons of gas. He also had aspi-

rations to compete in the transcontinental race that preceded the pylon events, so efforts were made to wet additional areas of the Bearcat's wings. However, he was unsuccessful in keeping fuel from leaking from the structure, so the idea of cross-country racing was abandoned.

The third pilot to fly a Bearcat in the 1964 National Championship Air Races was Czechoslovakian native Miroslav "Mira" Slovak. Prior to coming to the United States in 1953, Slovak had been a pilot for the government-controlled Czechoslovakian Airlines. For two years he carefully planned his escape from communist oppression. Then on March 23, 1953, while on a routine flight bound for Prague, he altered the flight plan and managed to defect to Frankfurt, West Germany. Ten years later Slovak was almost killed when the hydroplane he was racing at Idaho's Lake Coeur d'Alene disintegrated. Fortunately, he survived the accident, and in 1964 Bill Stead picked Slovak to race his Bearcat.

Navy pilot Lyle Shelton was detached to the Air Force and was serving as a T-38 flight instructor at

Bearcats in the Arizona desert west of Phoenix at the Navy's Litchfield Park storage yard. By the time this photo was taken in 1957, the U.S. Navy was exclusively flying jet-powered fighters. The Bearcats had been sitting in the desert from five to seven years, and were being sold cheaply to civilians or scrapped. (Brian Baker)

RACEPLANE **TECH**
SERIES

Ohlrich and Tonopah Queen *take the checkered flag for a fourth-place finish at the 1965 Las Vegas International Air Races at an average speed of 319.37 mph.* (Walt Ohlrich Collection)

Arizona Senator Barry Goldwater was running for president in 1964 and Greenamyer's unpainted racer featured a Goldwater elephant wearing glasses on its cowling. (Robert F. Pauley via Tim Weinschenker)

Randolph Air Force Base San Antonio, Texas, and he happened to be on extended leave from the military when he learned of the racing event. He then quickly caught an Air National Guard transport to Reno and had the good fortune to run into Clay Lacy, who needed some help preparing his Mustang for the upcoming race. Shelton lent Lacy a hand and later helped crew the airplane.

The turnout for the 1964 Unlimited Class was a disappointment for Bill Stead and his team, who had worked so hard to organize the event. The entry list had only seven airplanes, including four North American P-51D Mustangs and three Grumman F8F Bearcats. The environmental factors at Sky Ranch were very Spartan and unaccommodating. The all-dirt runways were unpaved and there were no proper facilities for the airplanes and pilots. "I was really appalled at the conditions of the runway at the small Sky Ranch Airport," recalled Ohlrich. "The longer runway near the hangar was dirt, a "no-no" for the thin, high-pressure tires on the Bearcat, and the other was too short for safety, but it did have Marston Matting. Bill Stead wanted the racers to take off and land at the ranch so ABC could film it for television. However, there were no facilities for servicing the planes there, so the decision was made for the Unlimiteds to take off from Reno Municipal, run the race, and then land at Sky Ranch for the television cameras before returning to the Reno Airport."

The racecourse mapped out at Sky Ranch measured 8.019 miles in

Mira Slovak flew the Bill Stead-owned F8F-2, N9885C, BuNo 121751, Race Number 80 during the 1964 and 1965 racing seasons. Slovak qualified sixth at the Los Angeles National Air Races, Lancaster, California, and placed third in the Championship Race, averaging 369.64 mph. (Emil Strasser via Gerry Liang)

Lyle Shelton flew Mike Carroll's Hawker Sea Fury (FB Mk.11, serial WG567) at Reno 1966. The aircraft is seen at Mojave, California, in its red and gold livery undergoing canopy modifications. The sprayed-out area on the tail is covering the aircraft's former Canadian registration, CF-VAN. (Nicholas A. Veronico Collection)

Race Number 1 featured several modifications in 1964. The most noticeable was its replacement canopy, which was fashioned from a searchlight dome from a Lockheed P2V Neptune patrol bomber. It is hard to say how much the canopy enhanced the racer's performance, but Greenamyer did capture the checkered flag in Reno's first heat race, only to be disqualified for not landing on the field for ABC's television coverage. (Robert F. Pauley via Tim Weinschenker)

Walt Ohlrich flew Tom Matthews' F8F-2, N7827C, BuNo 121752, Race Number 10, at the 1964 and 1965 Reno races. Ohlrich qualified fourth at 351.29 mph, flying what was essentially a stock Bearcat. The primitive conditions at the Reno Sky Ranch were tough on the aircraft, but great for spectators, as demonstrated by the carloads of enthusiasts standing near the barbed wire fence. (Walt Ohlrich Collection)

distance and each heat race consisted of 10 laps. The format for scoring the closed-course events was largely based on the points system that was used in hydroplane boat racing. Each aircraft was required to compete in two of four heat races, and points were awarded to each pilot in accordance to his respective finishing position. The Championship Race followed the heat competitions and the pilot with the highest cumulative points total would be declared the National Champion.

Korean War Ace Robert "Bob" Love, who was flying Chuck Lyford's P-51, was the top qualifier at 395.49 mph. Love was followed by Greenamyer's modified Bearcat, which qualified just ahead of Mira Slovak and Walt Ohlrich's F8Fs with average speed of 359.51 mph.

Walt Ohlrich's mount, Tonopah Queen; *Richard Weaver's P-51D N713DW, 45-11553, Race Number 15; and Darryl Greenamyer's Bearcat line the pit area at Lancaster in 1966. Ohlrich's Bearcat had been modified in the off-season with a P-51H spinner, a longer tail cone, and an updated water injection system. Ohlrich and Weaver placed fourth and fifth in the Unlimited Race.* (Walt Ohlrich Collection)

The first two heat races were held on September 18, 1964. Clay Lacy, flying his Mustang, *Bonzai*, won the first event; however, he was not the first to cross the finish line. That distinction went to Bob Love, who led the race from start to finish and posted a record 405-mph lap, but cut two pylons in the process. The resulting penalty dropped Love to third, behind Ohlrich's Bearcat. The second heat of the day featured the Bearcats flown by Slovak and Greenamyer pitted against Ben Hall's P-51D, *Seattle Miss*. Just as in the first heat, Greenamyer was the first to finish the race, but he did not actually win it. After capturing the checkered flag, Greenamyer briefly touched down on the runway but did not actually land at the ranch for the television people. He was later disqualified for not landing on the field, and that allowed Mira Slovak to officially claim the first win for a Grumman Bearcat.

Heats Three and Four were flown the following day. Bob Love's *Bardahl Special* won Heat Three, while Clay Lacy and Walt Ohlrich continued to race long after the finish. "The

starter flag was never in exactly the same place every race," said Ohlrich. "Clay Lacy and I both missed the checkered flag and just continued racing until we were low on fuel. We then both gave up and landed." Lacy actually came in second with Ohlrich's F8F finishing third. Only two airplanes competed in the last heat race of the event. Mira Slovak's *Smirnoff* F8F narrowly edged Ben Hall's Mustang for the win.

The high point of the 1964 Reno Air Races was the running of the Unlimited Championship Race on Sunday, September 20, 1964. Bob Love's top qualifying P-51 was the odds-on favorite; however, because of the points system, he would still need help in capturing the overall championship even if he won the race. To win, Love needed Slovak to either drop out of the race or to finish at the bottom of the pack. Unfortunately for Love that did not happen, because Slovak flew a very spirited competition and came in second with an average speed of 355.52 mph. Slovak's points totaled 1,100, compared to Love's 1,025. Looking back, it is apparent that Love's pylon cuts in Heat One clearly cost him the 1964 Unlimited Championship.

1965: NEW VENUES, MODIFICATIONS BEGIN

In spite of all of the problems that Bill Stead experienced in 1964, his efforts definitely raised interest in the sport of air racing. In addition to Reno, two new venues hosted Unlimited competitions in 1965. The first was officially called the Los Angeles National Air Races but was held at Fox Field in Lancaster, California. Darryl Greenamyer's F8F was undergoing major modifications so Bill Stead's Bearcat was the only Grumman to enter the race. Mira Slovak was again at the controls and won the first heat and placed third in the Championship Race. Chuck Lyford's fast Mustang was the overall winner with two heat victories plus a first-place finish in the Championship Race.

Greenamyer realized that his Bearcat would need additional work in order to compete with the likes of Lyford's *Bardahl Special*. After Reno 1964, he and his crew expended approximately 3,000 man-hours effecting the many changes that were made to his racer. The wingspan of Greenamyer's F8F was

A faulty blower seal manifested itself shortly after Greenamyer departed Burbank Airport for Reno. Greenamyer was unable to replace the bad seal in time for the races, so the aircraft lost approximately eight gallons of oil in each event. (Robert F. Pauley via Tim Weinschenker)

Walt Ohlrich flew Race Number 10 again during the 1965 racing season. For that season the aircraft was christened Tonopah Queen. (Walt Ohlrich Collection)

When Greenamyer won his third consecutive National Championship in 1967, his aircraft appeared in white paint with metallic blue trim. The Smirnoff logo was in black lettering, although in 1966 it had been metallic blue. An extra boil-off exhaust was added to the port side and equipment was added to the engine to inject nitromethane and water into the cylinder heads. (Emil Strasser via Gerry Liang)

Bob Kucera came to Reno in 1968 with his F8F-2, N212KA, BuNo 121528, Race Number 99. Kucera won the Unlimited Consolation Race with a speed of 331.851 mph, competing against three Mustangs, the F4U-4 Corsair of Gene Akers, and John Lear's A-26 Invader. Kucera was killed in the racer three months later, on December 13, 1968, at the Lost Nations Airport, Ohio. (William T. Larkins)

reduced by removing the factory designed outer wing panels. Grumman engineers had originally designed these panels to break away under heavy g-loads. By removing them, the wingspan was reduced from 35 feet to 27.5 feet, including the new wing tips that were designed by Lockheed engineer Mel Cassidy. The aircraft's landing flaps were also removed and the makeshift canopy was replaced with one that was similar to the type that was used on the Cosmic Wind Formula One racers. One of the most important aerodynamic changes that Greenamyer made to his Bearcat dealt with the cooling system.

Removing the Bearcat's wing-root oil coolers and covering their respective openings logically gave the aircraft less aerodynamic drag. However, the engine would still need some type of a cooling system.

Being a Lockheed test pilot gave Greenamyer access to some of the best engineering minds in the company. Lockheed engineer Pete Law designed a revolutionary boil-off type of oil cooling system for the Bearcat that consisted of a single DC-6 oil cooler, immersed in a boiler containing 10 gallons of antidetonant injection (ADI) fluid.

(text continued on page 73)

Chuck Klusman brought F8F-2, N148F, BuNo 121787, Race Number 11, to race at Reno 1966. The stock Bearcat qualified at 357.33 mph, won Heat 2, and finished fourth in the Unlimited Consolation Race at 342.74 mph. Klusman only raced the aircraft one year before selling it to John Church. (William T. Larkins)

John Church acquired N148F and began his racing career with the 1967 season. He finished second in the Unlimited Consolation Race with an average speed of 336.167 mph. Church also only raced the Bearcat one season before he sold it to Bud Fountain. Church returned to racing in 1970. (Emil Strasser via Gerry Liang)

ROUND-ENGINE RACERS

When air racing spectators compare the sleek, low drag frontal profile of a Merlin-powered racer, they often wonder how the flat-front radial engine-powered racers can be so fast. The brute horsepower developed by the R-3350 and R-4360 approaches a one horsepower to one cubic inch ratio, and that's the first secret to success. The second is airframe clean-up. Coupling reduced aerodynamic drag with a strong engine and an experienced pilot produces a winning combination.

Cook Cleland and teammates Dick Becker and Ben McKillen achieved the winning combination at the postwar Cleveland Air Races. Pilots like Darryl Greenamyer, Steve Hinton, and Lyle Shelton have battled the highly modified Mustangs on the circuit since 1969, when Chuck Hall arrived at Reno in *Miss R.J.* Each year the Unlimited Gold Race offers pilots and crews the opportunity to demonstrate their proficiency at fielding a racer. This is coupled with myriad outside factors, ranging from weather (winds and temperature), to engine reliability, to the competition, and plain old luck. All of the factors in air racing have seen round-engine racers in the winner's circle at Cleveland two out of the four postwar races, and at Reno 17 out of 37 times. At Reno, there is not always a competitive round-engine racer, but when there is, the competition is fierce.

This section of color pages serves as a trip through time, from the postwar Cleveland era to the mid-1960s – the days of races at the Reno Sky Ranch, and later Stead Field, to the years of dominance by racers with names such as *Conquest 1* and *Rare Bear*.

Cook Cleland's Lucky Gallon, *wearing a cream and red paint scheme, taxies out for the 1946 Thompson.* (Bernard Schulte)

Color photos of the postwar racing aircraft are very rare items indeed. Fortunately, Aaron King, who was a teenager at the time, decided to take some wonderful Kodachromes of Cook Cleland's winning F2G, as well as other 1949 racers, in order to have color reference for the future. (Aaron King)

The F2G truly dominated the National Air Races in 1949. Here is a very interesting shot of Cook Cleland's three F2Gs, lined left to right in the exact finishing order of the 1949 Thompson Trophy Race. (Aaron King)

Ron Puckett's beautiful F2G Miss Port Columbus, *on the Cleveland ramp, 1949. (Aaron King)*

Piloting this highly modified P-51 Mustang, Anson Johnson won the Thompson in 1948 and decided to defend his victory by removing the belly scoop from his aircraft and moving the coolant radiators to the leading edge of the wings. The results of Johnson's modification were not completely proven before he was forced to leave the Thompson competition in the ninth lap. (Aaron King)

The *Beguine* was one of the most interesting racers to have graced the post-World War II pylon events. Its emerald green paint was so shiny and so smooth that Bill Odom had to remove his shoes to gain entry to the cockpit. Note the yellow can on the ground near the wing tip. Cans of this type held water that was poured into each coolant pod in order to keep the engine from overheating while the aircraft was standing still. (Aaron King)

Ron Puckett was a dashing former World War II aviator who was not as well-funded or well-connected as front-runner Cook Cleland, but he was a fierce competitor. (Don Felton)

Gene Akers' Race Number 22 Lancer Two *heads up the line in the 1967 Reno Unlimited pits. Darryl Greenamyer won that year flying his Bearcat, Race Number 1,* Smirnoff *at an average speed of 392.62 mph. (Emil Strasser via Gerry Liang)*

Gary Meermans acquired FG-1D Wart Hog and renamed the aircraft Sky Boss. Assigned Race Number 111, Meermans qualified for Reno 1988 at 315.447 mph, too slow to make the field. (Nicholas A. Veronico)

Howard Pardue's rare XF8F-1 Bearcat, BuNo 90446, NL14HP, Race Number 14 was a competitive Unlimited Silver racer. The aircraft consistently flew 350-mph races. Pardue flew the diminutive racer in a tight line around the course and was a crowd favorite. (Nicholas A. Veronico)

Uncowled, the R-4360 is a monster. The Super Corsair crew worked miracles during the spring and summer of 1982, transforming the aircraft from hulk to finished racer in less than four months. Volunteers working 10 hours a day, seven days a week, fabricated the engine mount, cowling, and exhaust stacks. Steve Hinton flew the Super Corsair to first place in the 1985 Unlimited Gold Race. (Gerry Liang)

Bob Mitchem returned to Reno in 1970, his FG-1D N194G, BuNo 92050, Race Number 94, having undergone extensive modifications. Most visible was the engine change to an R-2800-CB-17 with a downdraft carburetor. (Gerry Liang)

Mira Slovak's F8F-2, N9885C, BuNo 121751, Race Number 80, is towed into the Unlimited pits at the Reno Sky Ranch, site of the races in both 1964 and 1965. Slovak and the Smirnoff Bearcat won the 1964 National Championship Air Races. (Emil Strasser via Gerry Liang)

Darryl Greenamyer's Race Number 1 Bearcat is seen at Mojave in 1976, shortly before its retirement to the National Air and Space Museum. (Gerry Liang)

Racing crews work late into the night, and all night when necessary. In 1988, Rare Bear's crew kept the engine running through the heat races, which enabled Lyle Shelton to push the engine to its fullest, resulting in a first place finish at an average speed of 456.821 mph. This was also Lyle Shelton's third Reno Gold victory. (Jim Dunn)

Late Saturday afternoon on race weekend 1991, both Lyle Shelton and Howard Pardue agreed to have their aircraft photographed together. The resulting photograph graphically illustrates the modifications made to Shelton's Rare Bear, *when compared to Pardue's stock Bearcat at right. (Jim Dunn)*

The Unlimited pits are a beehive of activity, and 1992 was no exception. This wide-angle view of the Rare Bear *pit presents rows of racers to the right and left, as well as the ramp fueling area in the distance.* (Nicholas A. Veronico)

The 1994 Unlimited field posed for an early morning photograph. The racers include, from front to rear: Rare Bear, Strega, Dago Red, Critical Mass, Baby Gorilla, Merlin's Magic, *and to the rear can be seen the noses of* Miss America *and* Dreadnought. *(Jim Dunn)*

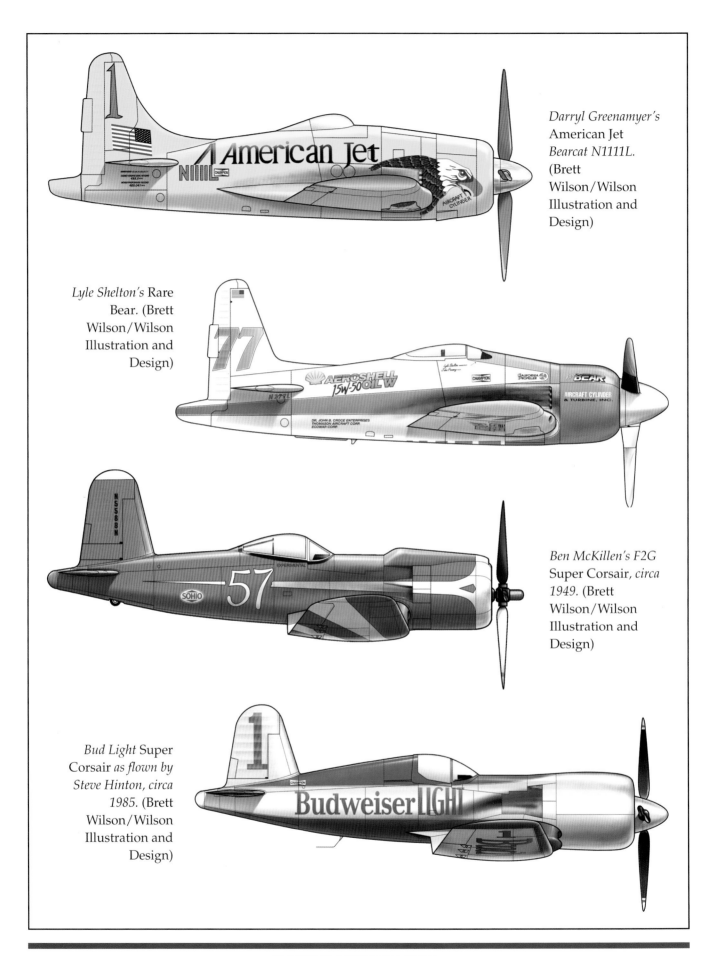

Darryl Greenamyer's American Jet *Bearcat N1111L.* (Brett Wilson/Wilson Illustration and Design)

Lyle Shelton's Rare Bear. (Brett Wilson/Wilson Illustration and Design)

Ben McKillen's F2G Super Corsair, *circa 1949.* (Brett Wilson/Wilson Illustration and Design)

Bud Light Super Corsair *as flown by Steve Hinton, circa 1985.* (Brett Wilson/Wilson Illustration and Design)

(text continued from page 64)

As the hot oil circulated through the cooler the ADI would burn off and be vented overboard through two small ports on the side of the fuselage. The level of fluid in the boiler was maintained with a float valve that was connected to the ADI pump, which also supplied the cooling mixture to the cylinder heads.

Weight reduction also played a key role in the future success of Greenamyer's Bearcat. The entire electrical system was removed from the aircraft and all of the racer's instruments were changed to direct reading types. The generator and heavy lead-acid 24-volt battery were replaced with a lightweight dry cell that powered the warning lights and radio. The hydraulic system was gutted with the exception of the main retract cylinders. The landing gear was retracted through the use of a 1,900-psi nitrogen bottle, and gravity was used as the lowering mechanism.

Next Greenamyer directed his attention to the Bearcat's engine and propeller configuration. The factory R-2800-34W engine was replaced with an R-2800–83W version, and a propeller that was originally designed for the R-3350-powered Douglas Skyraider supplanted the stock airscrew. The Skyraider propeller was approximately 12 inches longer than the standard Bearcat version. This afforded the F8F more propeller area but forced the pilot to make three-point takeoffs and landings, because the main gear was not long enough to give the propeller proper ground clearance. The nose case of the Pratt & Whitney R-2800-83W engine was upgraded with a nose case from an R-2800-44. This gave Greenamyer's racer a propeller-to-crankshaft ratio of 0.35:1, which translates to a propeller speed of only

980 rpm while the engine is running at 2,800 rpm. Lastly, a P-51H type spinner was fitted to the propeller.

For the 1965 Reno races, air-racing officials decided to allow the Unlimited pilots to stage their aircraft from the Reno Airport rather than have them land at Sky Ranch. Ten Unlimited Class aircraft turned out for the qualifying rounds. Greenamyer, Slovak, and Ohlrich where among those returning to compete. Also, future Championship Bearcat pilot Lyle Shelton had managed to get a racing slot flying P-51 *Tonopah Miss* for Richard Vartanian. Shelton accomplished his sudden rise to race pilot by advertising his services with business cards he left on warbirds at airports around southern California.

The modifications that Darryl Greenamyer made to his F8F instantly paid dividends at Reno, where he qualified number one, with an average speed of 369.70

mph. He also snared one heat race and came in second in another behind his rival, Chuck Lyford. At the same time Mira Slovak and Walt Ohlrich did not really push their Bearcats hard, because there was not much prize money in air racing at that time. Prize money at the time was not enough to pay for a new or overhauled engine.

On Sunday, September 12, 1965, three Mustangs and three Bearcats faced off for the second annual Unlimited Class Reno Championship Race. Darryl Greenamyer took the lead from the start with Chuck Lyford close behind, while Clay Lacy and Mira Slovak battled for third place. The duel between Greenamyer and Lyford initially stood up to the pre-race hype, until Lyford's engine backfired. Greenamyer then moved out so far in front of Lyford's Mustang that he could afford to pull the power back and cruise to an easy win. Lacy managed to hold off Slo-

On August 16, 1969 Darryl Greenamyer piloted his Conquest 1 to a New World record of 483.041 mph. The attempt was made at Edwards Air Force Base located in California's Mojave Desert. During the four runs across the measured course, an exhaust leak pushed the cockpit temperature to nearly 200 degrees Fahrenheit, and Greenamyer suffered burns on his hands. A few weeks later Greenamyer also captured his fifth Reno National Championship. (William T. Larkins via Tim Weinschenker)

We are very fortunate that team member Pete Behenna had the presence of mind to photo document the rebuilding of Shelton's Bearcat. This particular photo clearly shows the complexity of such a task that faces the crew as it went through each of the aircraft's systems. The gun blisters were removed and the gun holes on the leading edge of the wings were covered and smoothed. (Pete Behenna via Neal Nurmi)

It took Shelton and his crew only nine months to get the racer ready for Reno 1969. Along the way, Shelton bought many the of much needed parts and later learned that, in some cases, the parts he had purchased had originally been stolen from the Grumman fighter while it sat derelict in Indiana. Here Race Number 70 has it wings attached, is on its gear, and has the new engine mount installed. (Pete Behenna via Neal Nurmi)

vak, who finished fourth. Ohlrich and Shelton were flying stock aircraft that really couldn't compete with the frontrunners, so they rounded out the race finishing fifth and sixth respectively.

Two weeks after winning Reno, Greenamyer was ready to compete in his third Unlimited meet of the year. During qualifying, he went out and broke Chuck Brown's 1948 pylon speed record of 418.30 mph by posting an average speed of 423.40 mph. Lyford's Mustang also flew faster at Las Vegas, clocking 418.14 mph.

Lyford and Greenamyer dominated the four heat races just as they had in Reno a few weeks before. Greenamyer easily won his two heats, while Lyford won one and dropped out of the second during the seventh lap of the 10-lap, 93.5-mile race. The Championship Race again featured three P-51s and three F8Fs. Through seven laps the two top qualifiers were neck-and-neck, with the lead changing on almost every lap. Then Greenamyer began to fall back and finally departed the race in the ninth lap. Greenamyer's

At Left: Lyle Shelton (center) working on the outer wing panel of his racer. At Right: Shelton's first engine was a Wright R-3350-26W that had been exposed to the elements for some time. However, the engines internal workings were in good shape. (Pete Behenna via Neal Nurmi)

race strategy was to shift his R-2800-83A engine into high blower if Lyford began to pull away. To do so, he needed to reduce the power to prevent the manifold pressure from surging. Unfortunately, the power was not pulled back enough when Greenamyer made the shift and about a half lap later, the engine backfired and lifted the top of the cowling.

1966–1969: GREENAMYER'S YEARS OF DOMINATION

In 1966, Greenamyer installed a supercharger from an R-2800-CB-17 in his Bearcat. The larger supercharger boosted his engine power to 2,500 horsepower, but the added weight, coupled with the weight of the boil-off cooling system, made the racer nose heavy. So, the boiler was relocated from in front of the pilot to an area behind the cockpit. Greenamyer also removed 18 inches from the vertical tail and rudder and installed an after spinner fairing from a Lockheed Constellation behind the propeller in order to better streamline the frontal engine area of the racer. The aircraft was then painted gloss white with metallic blue arrows on the wings and fuselage.

The Los Angeles National Air Races offered the first Unlimited competition of 1966. As in 1965, the actual racing events were again staged in Lancaster. Greenamyer brought his newly painted Race Number 1 to the meet, but he quickly discovered that his aircraft was difficult to control at high speeds. Greenamyer had intended to not only race at Lancaster, but he also wanted to make an attempt to break the world's speed record for a piston engine airplane. However, the reduced tail surfaces drastically affected the stability of the racer, so Greenamyer pulled out of the Los Angeles event and aborted his attempt at the speed record.

In 1966, the National Championship Air Races were moved from Sky Ranch to the recently decommissioned Stead Air Force Base, about 10 miles north of Reno. The base had been named after Bill Stead's brother, Croston, who was killed in an accident while flying with the Nevada National Guard. This new location gave the event coordinator plenty of room for the fans and competitors. Sadly, Bill Stead, who had worked so hard to revive air racing was not around to see the sport's new home, as he was killed in April 1966 while flying a Formula 1 racer near Tampa, Florida. It was also in 1966 when the points system was abandoned in favor of using the qualifying positions to determine the placement of aircraft in the final races of the Reno event. This system had the advantage of getting the fastest airplanes in the Championship Race; however, it made the outcome of preceding heat races meaningless.

Prior to Reno 1966, Greenamyer borrowed a vertical tail and rudder from Bill Fornoff. The new tail assembly added the stability to an aircraft that was already tuned to perfection. Greenamyer went on to dominate the Reno races by capturing the top qualifying position in addition to winning every race, including the all-important Championship Race. Over the next three years, Greenamyer and his Bearcat continued their reign as National Champions by posting consecutive wins in 1967, 1968, and 1969. In 1969, Darryl Greenamyer also made a successful attempt at the long-standing three-kilometer (Km) world speed record.

In 1939, Flugkapitän Fritz Wendel established the new speed record for a piston-powered aircraft while flying a Messerschmitt Me 209 at 469.2 mph. Since that time, no one had come close to breaking Wendel's mark, but on August 16, 1969, Greenamyer made four passes at 510.23, 458.85, 508.46 and 454.62 mph, over the three-kilometer course that had been laid out on the dry lakebed near Edwards Air Force Base, California. The average speed of the four consecutive passes was 483.041 mph—a new world's speed record.

Lyle Shelton enjoying the victory parade after winning the Cape May Championship Race. The only visible modification made to Race Number 77 was a replacement spinner from a Northrop P-61. (Pete Behenna via Neal Nurmi)

Ron Reynolds and Mike Geren co-owned F8F-2 N5005, BuNo 121731, Race Number 44, which Reynolds flew in both the 1970 Harold's Club Trophy Dash and the Reno closed-course races. En route from Milwaukee during the Trophy Dash, Reynolds encountered freezing rain and deadsticked into Sioux City, Iowa. He got the racer to Reno, where he qualified at 349.714 mph, and placed second. (William T. Larkins)

Gunther Balz enjoyed flying his stock Bearcat (F8F-1, N9G, BuNo 90454), and simultaneously owned and campaigned the highly modified P-51D Roto-Finish Special *(see RaceplaneTech Series, Volume 1). Balz flew the Bearcat in both the 1970 Harold's Club Trophy Dash and the Reno pylon races. He finished second in the Trophy Dash, and fifth in the Unlimited Championship Race. (William T. Larkins)*

During the 1966–1969 period, Lyle Shelton also had made great strides as a race pilot and eventually as an owner of a racing Bearcat. Shelton moved from crewing Clay Lacy's Mustang in 1964 to racing a P-51D Mustang for Glenn Hussey in 1965 and a Hawker Sea Fury in 1966 for Mike Carroll. The racing bug had severely bitten Shelton, and he began to look for an airplane of his own when Walt Ohlrich told him about a wrecked F8F that was standing derelict at Valparaiso, Indiana.

The Bearcat in question was Grumman F8F-2, BuNo 122629, which had been surplused by the U.S. Navy in May 1958 to Stinson Field Aircraft of San Antonio, Texas for $788.91. The aircraft was registered with the FAA as N1031B. In October 1962, N1031B was heavily damaged and more or less abandoned at Valparaiso, Indiana. Earl Reinert, who in turn resold what was left of the aircraft to Mike Couches, purchased the wreckage of the Bearcat. N1031B finally found a permanent home after Lyle Shelton bought the future racer in May 1968.

Shelton took the aircraft apart and transported it to hangar F8 at the Compton Airport in California, where he and his crew chief, Cliff Putman, and engineer Bill Hickle began the rebuilding process. Along the way crewmember Pete Behenna documented the rebuilding process on film. The most immediate need was parts, so Shelton started buying and borrowing from people around the country. The tail section and the control stick were acquired from Bob Kucera's ill-fated F8F (N212KA, BuNo 121528, crashed December 13, 1968). Shelton later discovered that many of the parts he was purchasing had originally been stolen from the Bearcat while it was in Indiana. From the beginning, Shelton believed that an R-3350-powered Bearcat was the path to winning championships, so he procured an engine, which had been out in the weather for some time. In a period of approximately 12 months, Shelton and his companions transformed the bucket of Bearcat parts into a racing machine that was ready for its first run-up. "I can remember the first ground run," recalled Shelton's son, John Slack. "All kinds of stuff came out of that

engine when it was started, but it smoothed out and ran fine after about an hour of running time."

By midsummer Shelton was ready to fly the aircraft; however, he was having some difficulty in getting the plane registered with the FAA. Shelton stated in a letter to the FAA: "I have bet $20,000 of copilot wages that it will fly at Reno, 19–22 Sept. 1969. And I hope to test fly the machine before I leave on two weeks USNR active duty on 23 August 1969. So you can see that I need a number in a very short time to do this." Shelton received N777L as his registration number, but only had time to fly the aircraft twice before it was time to head for Reno. Shelton's less-than-glamorous looking Bearcat, named *The Able Cat,* finally made it to Reno. It qualified sixth, ahead of three other F8Fs that were piloted by Gunther Balz (F8F-1, N9G, BuNo 90454), Walt Ohlrich (F8F-2, N7827C, BuNo 121752), and Bud Fountain (F8F-2, BuNo 121787). Shelton's racer also came in third in Heat Two and placed fifth in the Championship Race, easily won by Darryl Greenamyer.

1970–1975
The Racing Field Expands

The Seventh Annual National Championship Air Races were once again staged at Stead Field near Reno, Nevada, during September 15–17, 1970. In the off-season, Shelton installed a new reduction gear system in his Bearcat's engine. The 988TC18EA-2 nose case came from a commercial Wright R-3350 engine of the type used on Lockheed's Constellation. This new engine-to-propeller gear ratio allowed the Skyraider M20A-162 blades to turn more efficiently, producing more thrust with the same engine power. This modification put Shelton's racer on equal terms with Darryl Greenamyer's R-2800-powered *Conquest I.* Four Bearcat pilots qualified for the Unlimited competitions, including Greenamyer and Shelton, as well as Gunther Balz in his F8F-1 *Roto-Finish Bearcat* and Ron Reynolds in his F8F-2 (N5005, BuNo121731) Race Number 44, which he co-owned with Michael Geren.

Both Balz and Reynolds entered what would be the last Harold's Club Trophy Dash, from Milwaukee, Wisconsin, to Reno, Nevada, a distance of 1,667 miles. The Harold's Club Trophy Dash was run on September 13, prior to the pylon competition, and the Bearcats of Balz and Reynolds competed against a field of five other P-51D Mustangs. "Geren had a large belly tank, and we decided to enter the Bearcat in the Milwaukee-to-Reno transcontinental race," said Reynolds. "We didn't have any intention of flying the airplane around pylons when we entered the race. When the racers were taking off at Milwaukee, the weather was crappy, with a storm covering most of the central United States. Some of the pilots who had long-range tanks and lots of IFR (Instrument Flight Rules)

capability were able to climb out on top, and fly, I guess, nonstop to Reno. I, of course, could not do that—even with the belly tank. I was fifth in the takeoff sequence and headed for Reno with a stop planned for Rock Springs, Wyoming.

"I got into freezing rain and was 400 miles or so west of Milwaukee when the engine quit. In the Bearcat there is an alternate air door that bypasses the normal induction system that allows hot air to go to the engine in case of ice. On the Bearcat, there's a little 'T' handle on a cable that you pull out from the instrument panel. I pulled and yanked, and I had both feet on the instrument panel pulling on that handle and couldn't get it to budge. It was frozen solid—not by ice, but crud and from never being used probably. So I'm on instruments and I called a "mayday.' I began spiraling down through the overcast, and the controllers at Sioux City, Iowa, answered my mayday call. They wanted to know my last known position, which was on the airway just south of their airport—fortu-

nately. I spiraled down from 8,000 feet to 700 feet and broke out a couple hundred feet over the approach lights, lined up for the north-south runway. What luck! I had no radios tuned in, nothing. I just spiraled down, broke out, and as I descended into warmer air, the ice from the windshield cleared, enabling me to see the runway. That was the end of my transcontinental racing career. The engine was OK, it was just an icing problem. I got to Reno long after the race was over, and because we had no income from the transcontinental race's purse, we made the decision to take the tank off and run it in the heat races."

While Reynolds was thankful to be on the ground at Sioux City, Balz was winging his way to Reno. He flew the course in six hours, and 5.5 minutes at an average speed of 273.45 mph, placing second behind Dick Kestle (five hours, 52.4 minutes, 283.66 mph) in his P-51D *Miss Royal Crown Cola.*

Greenamyer had retired his racer to a museum after setting the world's speed record, but he

Jack Sliker taxies out for the Unlimited Race at Mojave 1974 in Escape II. *He finished fourth at 369.504 mph. (Nicholas A. Veronico Collection)*

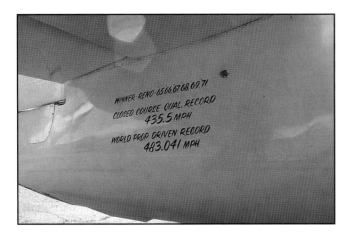
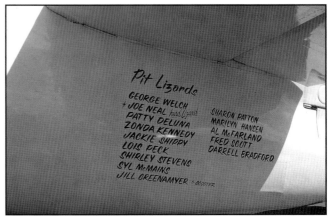

Under horizontal detail of Conquest I, starboard and port sides. (Gerry Liang)

showed up with it at Reno anyway. He qualified second behind Clay Lacy's purple P-51. Shelton won Heat One with an average speed of 369.268 mph. Heat Two was won by Mike Loening's P-51D, but Gunther Balz's F8F-1 managed to narrowly defeat Greenamyer's *Conquest I* for second place. The Harrah's Championship Race featured four Mustangs and three Bearcats, but the F8Fs did not fair very well on the race course. Greenamyer's one-shot, gas-driven gear retraction system did not pull his right landing gear all the way into the wheel well, so he pulled away from the racers that were forming up on Bob Hoover's pace plane and quickly landed at the field. His crew hurriedly changed out the nitrogen bottle and Greenamyer quickly took-off to rejoin the start of the race. Unfortunately, the new gas bottle did not fix the problem, so Greenamyer flew the race with his right gear partially exposed. Shortly after the start, Shelton's Bearcat experienced an engine failure. "I had the pole position for the start, and the engine failed when power was added, due to big overdose of nitro methane mixture, suggested by the Champion Spark Plug people," said Shelton. "I landed a little high and fast on the north-south runway in front of the grandstand, but I felt I had plenty of runway. But Bob Hoover kept saying 'ground loop it' over the radio. I didn't see why, but I hit the right brake anyway and blew a tire and ground looped the aircraft with plenty of room to spare. At that point I decided that I was going to make my own decisions and not listen to a guy who was 1,000 feet above me." Lacy went on to win the competition, and Balz, flying the lone Bearcat, finished in fifth position. In the Unlimited Consolation Race, Reynolds finished a close second behind Sherman Cooper's *Miss Merced* Sea Fury.

Bearcats were entered in four Unlimited Races in 1971. The first event was held at Cape May County Airport, New Jersey, during June 2–6. Shelton's Bearcat, Race Number 77, won $250 by posting the top qualifying speed of 361.93 mph (slower speed because the competition was run at sea level). Balz's F8F-1 was the only other Bearcat to enter the event and it qualified in eighth position. Four heat races were run leading up to the money rounds that were held on June 6. Balz won the first heat, but Clay Lacy's Mustang dominated the remaining three races. In the final race, Shelton's Bearcat, now named *Phoenix I*, led from start to finish and easily won the competition. Balz came in third in addition to placing eighth in the Consolation Race.

Sliker and Mac McClain await the signal to take off for the 1974 Unlimited Gold Race at Mojave. The Red Baron *was later fitted with a Griffon engine, driving counter-rotating propellers, and it dominated the racing circuit during the last half of the decade. (Gerry Liang)*

The second Unlimited competition of 1971 featured a 1,000-mile race of endurance. It was held at Brown Field near San Diego, California, on July 18, 1971. Sixteen aircraft, including two Bearcats—flown by Shelton and Reynolds—entered the 100-lap race. Shelton qualified his race-modified Grumman F8F-2 at 324.4 mph, but in a long race, speed is not as important as finishing the 1,000 miles, so Shelton's *Phoenix I* was equipped with underwing fuel tanks to increase its range. Shelton started with the first set of four aircraft to take to the course. Korean War Ace Bob Love took the early lead, but in the end Sherman Cooper's Sea Fury *Miss Merced* was the only aircraft that completed the 100 laps. Shelton placed fourth. The race ended tragically for Ron Reynolds, when he lost his long-time friend and racing partner, Mike Geren.

"We had preprogrammed four pit stops at San Diego. Geren and I were going to alternate flying responsibilities, and we had agreed that I would start the race," Ron Reynolds said. "I flew 19 laps and then came in for a pit stop. The crew fueled the aircraft, added oil, I got out and Mike got in. I strapped him in, and he reentered the race. You get caught up in the heat of the race and you do some absolutely crazy things. Collectively, we should have made the decision to pull out of the race at the first pit stop. The engine was consuming an unbelievable amount of oil. I do not know if we were about to lose a cylinder or what. The R-2800 can lose a cylinder and it will not show up on the cylinder head temperature gauge or give any other indication of failure. We were running the engine wide open, but no oil was being thrown onto the windshield. It was being blown out the back and through the breather. At the pit stop we added 12

Ron Reynolds down low on the course at the 1971 U.S. Cup at Brown Field, near San Diego, California. Later in the day, Mike Geren was killed while attempting to land this aircraft after the engine lost a fuel line that started a fire. (Gerry Liang)

or 15 gallons, and we should have stopped right then."

"Mike was a good pilot, but a fuel line broke on the airplane and that started a fire. Then the master rod let go and wiped out a bunch of cylinders," Reynolds said, remembering his friend. "By this time Mike had a fire with smoke coming into the cockpit through the wing root air ducts. Mike leveled off on the downwind leg like he was making a routine landing. He turned to base and then dropped the gear, which is the worst thing he could have done under the circumstances. Mike was trying to save the airplane, and as soon as he put the gear down, the fuselage was enveloped by smoke. I'm sure that's when he was asphyxiated." Mike Geren rode the Bearcat in at a 30-degree angle and perished. Reynolds continued racing, serving as a check airman at Reno for a number of years. He went on to acquire another Bearcat, the last F8F-2 built, BuNo 122708 (N7701C) that was eventually sold to Jack Sliker. Reynolds had retired from racing by 1975.

For the 1971 Reno races, officials dropped the elliptical race course that had served them since 1964. In its place an eight-pylon, nonsymmetrical, slightly longer 9.815-mile lap was laid out over the desert floor around Stead Field. The new course greatly influenced the outcome of the qualifying rounds, as six out of 18 aircraft registered speeds of more than 400 mph. Shelton's *Phoenix I* took the second starting position, qualifying at 418.009 mph, while Greenamyer's *Conquest I* placed fourth at 405.984 mph. Ohlrich rounded out the Bearcat entries in the 10th starting position. None of the competitors, including the powerful Bearcats, flew faster than the 419.501 mph posted by Gunther Balz's *Roto Finish*, a highly modified Mustang. For the first time in Reno air racing history, it now appeared that there were at least two aircraft capable of breaking Darryl Greenamyer's reign as Unlimited Champion.

Shelton and Greenamyer went head-to-head in Heat 1-B. Greenamyer's Bearcat had a new engine but Shelton won the first meeting by nar-

This photo clearly depicts the amount of oil that is exhausted from the racer's powerful R-3350 engine. (Pete Behenna via Neal Nurmi)

rowly defeating *Conquest I*. Shelton's victory set the stage for Sunday's Classic Championship Race.

Mike Loening's Mustang took the early lead in the Championship Race, but after lap two his engine let go. All of the race pilots, with the exception of Greenamyer, responded to Loening's emergency by pulling up to 500 feet. Balz and Shelton then assumed first and second positions for a short time, before Greenamyer passed Shelton. Greenamyer, remaining low on the course, made his move in the fourth lap and passed Balz, while Sherman Copper's Sea Fury moved ahead of Shelton and Balz. Shelton then passed both Balz

and Cooper and moved in behind Greenamyer. Shelton was right on Greenamyer's tail as the two Bearcats passed the finish line. "On the last lap, as we came down the straightaway to finish, Greenamyer moved out to the absolute edge of the course, so I couldn't pass him without violating the deadline," recalled Shelton. Greenamyer had won his sixth Reno Unlimited Championship; however, many felt that he had flown too low and clearly had failed to pull up to the required 500-foot level during the two emergency situations. Shelton filed a protest against Greenamyer, but the Contest Committee disallowed the protest and instead fined the six-time champion $750 for the three race violations. The committee's decision that day didn't sit very well with Shelton's crew, but it certainly added fuel to the rivalry that already existed between Shelton and Greenamyer.

In 1972, Shelton's Bearcat, with its new name, *Phast Phoenix*, was again pitted against *Conquest I*, which was being flown by Richard Laidley. During qualifying the low-cut canopy that was developed by Shelton's crew departed the aircraft and struck and damaged the vertical tail. A stock replacement was borrowed from Bud Fountain's Bearcat, and Shelton managed to place second in the Championship Race, behind Balz's front-running P-51 *Roto Finish Special*.

Lyle Shelton started 1973 off right by winning the Roscoe Turner Speed Classic competition at the Great Miami Air Race. Eight months later Shelton's Bearcat, *US Thrift 7 1/4% Special*, set a new record of 426.602 mph while qualifying for Reno National Championship Air Races. Race Number 77 also defeated Cliff Cummins' P-51D in the Unlimited Championship Race while posting an average speed of

Shelton was sponsored by a Phoenix bank in 1973 and hence the name US Thrift Assn. 7 1/4% Special. *Race Number 77 set a new qualification speed of 426.602 mph and also came in first in the Reno Championship Race. (Bill LeSauche via Neal Nurmi)*

428.155 mph, which was also a Reno record. At Mojave, Shelton easily won the race with an average speed of 396.614 mph. Sadly, as the race was concluding, Bud Fountain's F8F-2 *Hawke Dusters* (N148F, BuNo 121787) began to trail black smoke. The aircraft clawed for altitude before winging over and impacting the ground, killing Fountain. In October, Shelton won his third Unlimited championship of the year by capturing the California Air Classic, which was held at Mojave.

Reno 1974 began for Lyle Shelton just as it had in 1973. His renamed *Omni Special* Bearcat again established a new qualifying record of 432.252 mph and easily won the first heat race as well. The *Omni Special* was the clear front-runner in 1974 and Shelton did not let his fans down. He not only set a new course speed of 431 mph but also outdistanced second-place finisher Ken Burnstine in P-51 *Miss Suzi Q* by more than 50 mph. After the race, the Contest Committee held up the prize money as it determined what to do about Shelton's failure to climb to a safe height during two maydays and Bob Love's altitude violation at the finish line. "Bob Love finished second with an ailing engine that forced him to reach for additional altitude at the end of the last lap," said Shelton. "I was way out in front and the mayday was behind me so there was no interference. Three or four weeks later the Contest Committee finally informed me that I was being dropped from first to fifth place for not pulling up to the 500-foot altitude during the mayday. Love was also dropped from second to sixth for exceeding the maximum altitude at the finish line." Shelton protested the ruling and again explained that he did not hear the distress calls because his radio was malfunctioning, but the race officials

Mike Smith bought the former Bill Stead F8F-2, BuNo 121751, repainted the aircraft, named it Lois Jean, *and changed the racing number to 41. Smith's engine went south after losing an oil line during qualifying. He was able to change the engine out in time for another attempt. He posted a speed of 352.096 mph, qualifying 13th. During the Unlimited Medallion Race, Smith finished second behind Ken Burnstine in the P-51* Miss Suzy Q. *Both were disqualified for flying outside the course deadline.* (Gerry Liang)

dismissed his objection. This was the second time in four years that Shelton had been denied the win due to a course violation. Some race historians feel that the Reno officials were somehow politically motivated to rule against Shelton. Whatever the case may be, it is interesting to note that the 500-foot emergency rule was eliminated in 1975 when the Professional Race Pilots Association took over officiating, using its revised rules of competition.

Losing the Championship Race in 1974 left Shelton's crew very angry and unsatisfied. At Mojave the following year, Greenamyer and Shelton were again the top two qualifiers. Shelton exacted some revenge over Greenamyer by finishing ahead of *Conquest I* in the Championship Race, but Cliff Cummins' P-51, *Miss Candace*, bested both of the fast Bearcats. A few months later, Greenamyer's Race Number 1 set a new speed record at Reno by qualifying at 435.556 mph. Shelton also set a record in the 1975 Champi-

onship Race, which he also happened to win with an average speed of 429.916 mph. Greenamyer attempted to start the competition, but a faulty prop governor prevented his Bearcat from generating enough power to take off. By winning the race, Shelton became the second person to win more than one Reno Championship. There would certainly be more wins in Shelton's future, and one more for Greenamyer as well, but 1975 marked the last time that Race Number 1 would compete on a pylon course. In 1977, Darryl Greenamyer donated his record-setting Bearcat to the Smithsonian Institution's National Air & Space Museum.

1976–1988
YEARS OF CONSOLIDATION

The year 1976 began a period when very few Bearcats competed on the racecourses around the country. It was also a year that started a long string of bad luck for Lyle Shelton.

The fourth annual California National Air Races were the first Unlimited event for the bicentennial of the United States of America. Twelve pilots brought their racing machines to Mojave to race around the 8.5-mile course. Shelton's Bearcat, renamed *Spirit of '77,'* was late getting to Mojave and during the qualifying period had an engine failure, which forced Shelton to make a wheels-up landing. "An improperly installed oil line came loose and starved the back side of the engine," recalled Shelton. "I pulled up and around and was approaching the main runway when the supercharger drive froze and then sheared. The engine shut down instantly. I dropped the gear handle at about 500 feet and checked the gear indicators and saw barber poles. At about the same time, some guy on the radio yelled that my gear wasn't down. I jerked the manual release but did not have enough time to get the gear down before I ran out of airspeed and altitude in the flair. You see, I wasn't getting any hydraulic pressure from the

engine pump and the accumulator for my hydraulic system had bled down prior to the race. (We were going to fix the accumulator after the run.)"

Lyle's son, John Slack, remembered the faulty oil line was, in fact, attached to the engine with an automotive hose clamp that was loosened by engine vibration. Bill Hickle, Lyle's engineer and quality control expert, was not at Mojave due to a car accident, and the mistake made in his absence put the aircraft out of racing until 1980.

During Shelton's four-year absence, a number of Bearcats showed up on the racing circuit. Basically stock, these aircraft and their pilots were enjoying a sport of speed. Bill Whittington arrived at Reno 1977 with his F8F-2 (N7827C, BuNo 121752) formerly owned by Thomas Matthews and later Walt Ohlrich. Whittington qualified 13th at 350.70 mph, and flew to a fifth-place finish in Heat 1A at a speed of 307.92 mph. He was fast enough to qualify for the Unlimited Consolation Race, which he placed fourth,

flying at 330.75 mph. The following year, John Herlihy showed up for Reno in Race Number 98, an F8F-2 (N198F, BuNo 122637), which had previously been owned and raced by John Church. Herlihy qualified at 358.67 mph, 12th overall, and went on to win the Unlimited Consolation Race at 368.58 mph. Herlihy was the sole Bearcat again at Reno in 1979, where he went on to place third in the Unlimited Silver at 359.31 mph.

Bill Whittington came back to Reno in 1980 with both his F8F-2 and his Race Number 09 *Precious Metal,* in which he qualified first at 421.61 mph. He qualified the Bearcat at an average speed of 335.98. Lyle Shelton returned to pylon racing in 1980 with a newly decorated Race Number 77 named *Rare Bear.* The unique label originated from a phone call between Shelton and well-known air race historian John Tegler. "Tegler had called Lyle while they were getting the plane ready for Reno," recalled Slack. "He mentioned to Lyle that the plane should be called *Rare Bear,* and the name stuck." *Rare Bear,* indeed, as it was one of only two Bearcats to show up for Reno in 1980. However, Shelton's streak of bad luck was far from over.

During Gold Heat Race One, *Rare Bear* experienced a hydraulic leak in the cockpit. The following day Shelton got in line to start Gold Heat Race Two but could not retract his right landing gear and was having radio problems at the same time. He finally got the gear situation sorted out just as the other pilots were headed down the chute and entering the course. Shelton put the fuel to his powerful R-3350 and soon began to pass slower competitors. Then in the fifth lap his blower system failed and he was out of the race. This time the race committee did Shelton a favor by officially listing him as a "Did Not

Shelton had named his aircraft Phoenix I *and equipped it with external fuel tanks for the 1971 U.S. Cup Race. Shelton completed 88 laps on the 10-mile course and finished the race in fourth place with a lapsed time of 3:2:27.8. (Gerry Liang)*

Start" (DNS), rather than disqualifying him for starting a race without a functioning radio.

In 1981 things started to look up for Shelton and his crew. *Rare Bear* qualified sixth with an average speed of 416.037 mph and beat Skip Holm in P-51D *Jeannie* in Gold Heat Race One. However, a burnt piston in Gold Heat Race Four again put number 77 out of the competition. The only positive news for fans of the Grumman F8F Bearcat came from Don Whittington, who won the 1981 Bronze Race in *Bearcat Bill*.

Rare Bear did not compete in 1982 but did return the following year. Shelton increased the Bear's speed to 432.047 mph and qualified in fifth position. He also finished third in both Gold Heat Races, giving him a nice starting position for the final competition on Sunday, September 18, 1983. Shelton cut a pylon while struggling with a rough-running engine in the Gold Race. He continued to fly and was in third place on the eighth lap before he finally declared a mayday. He landed safely on Runway 14, but blew a tire in the process. Later he learned that he had crossed the race deadline while handling the many things that were happening to his airplane during the race. The penalty for the deadline breach resulted in disqualification.

One of the rarest of Bearcats turned up at Reno in 1983. Howard Pardue of Breckenridge, Texas, had acquired XF8F-1 (N14HP, BuNo 90446) from George Enhorning and came west to go racing. Wearing Race Number 14, Pardue qualified the stock Bearcat at a respectable 375.75 mph. He would qualify the Bearcat within 12 miles plus or minus every year through 1999. The aircraft was a consistent Silver racer, usually placing in the top three spots. Pardue flies the little

Darryl Greenamyer returned to air racing after a two-year absence. He posted the top qualifying speed at both California National Air Races and the Reno National Championship Air Races but was unable to win either of the two races. (Emil Strasser via Gerry Liang)

Grumman fighter in a tight line around the course, and is very competitive. Pardue and the Bearcat are a crowd favorite.

1985–1987 NEW RIVALRIES FOR *RARE BEAR*

Rare Bear was out of racing in 1984; however, 1985 marked the first of many classic battles between Shelton's R-3350-powered racer and the Mustang known as *Strega*.

Bill "Tiger" Destefani first brought *Strega* to Reno in 1983, but the plane was plagued with problems and, consequently, it did not finish any of the races it started. The following year a burnt piston forced pilot Ron Hevle to leave the race in the seventh lap. But in 1985 it appeared that Tiger had worked the bugs out of his Rolls-Royce-powered racer and for the first time was truly ready to compete for the Gold.

The first Unlimited Air Race of the 1985 was held in Bakersfield, California, over the first weekend in June. The two-day event featured

Unlimited Silver and Gold heat races, as well as two final races for the trophy. Shelton had his Bearcat running fairly well and registered a qualifying speed of 418.774 mph, but it was only good enough for third position. Mustangs flown by Ron Hevle and Skip Holm placed ahead of Shelton with respective speeds of 431.451 mph and 421.172 mph. Shelton finished second in the Gold Heat Race, behind Ron Hevle flying *Strega*.

"Bob Love was flying the pace plane that day," recalled Shelton. "He took us about five miles south of Minter Field and we all lined up for the start, as Love put us in a fairly high speed dive. At that point the Bearcat started to porpoise on me, so I pulled the power back. (We had an aft CG problem with the plane.) I was in last place about a half-mile back of the pack when Love officially started the race. As I went into the first turn, I pulled back and, all of a sudden, I got a neutral stick, which will scare the hell out of you. I had to push the stick forward with a con-

The Whittington brothers, Don and Bill, became the owners of F8F-2 BuNo 121752 in late 1977. Bill flew the aircraft at the 1979 Miami International Air Races at Homestead, Florida, which the brothers promoted. This aircraft began racing in 1964, when it was owned by Tom Matthews and flown by Walt Ohlrich. (John Kirk)

One of the rarest stock Bearcats, Howard Pardue's XF8F-1 NL14HP, BuNo 90446, began its racing career in 1983. Pardue raced the aircraft until it was damaged at Oshkosh. Race 14 was a crowd favorite in the Unlimited Silver and Bronze classes for the way Pardue competed in the plane. (Shawn Aro)

siderable amount of force in a 4- to 5-g turn to keep the airplane from pitching up and going out of control. Looking back, I probably should have pulled out of the race, but I finally figured out that as I approached the turns I would roll a great deal of down trim while holding back on the stick. When I would go into the turn, I would not run out of back stick. As I came out of the turn I would have to reverse the trim to keep from pitching down as I rolled out and unloaded the airplane. I got better at it as the race went on, and I started to catch Hevle, but I never did."

Three months later *Rare Bear* showed up at Reno with John Penney at the controls. Penney was a highly experienced aviator, former Air Force pilot, and test pilot for the Lear Fan Corp., but he was still a rookie when it came to air racing. Reno 1985 was a record-breaking year for the Unlimited Class, as all nine of the top qualifiers posted speeds greater than 422 mph. Penney qualified *Rare Bear* in seventh position with an average speed of 429.485 mph, which was less than

one mile an hour slower than *Strega*.

The mission of all of the top qualifiers is to get into the Gold Race on the final day of Reno. The top three qualifiers were automatically in, but the rest of the field had to go out and win their corresponding heats in order to earn a start in the final race. John Penney accomplished that feat in Heat Race 1-A by leading the competition from start to finish. A very promising start came to a sudden end the following day, when an oil plug that was not safety wired, dropped off *Rare Bear's* engine in the last lap of Heat 2-A. Without lubricant, the engine quickly seized, grounding Penney for the balance of the race week. Top qualifier Neil Anderson in *Dreadnought*, an R-4360-powered Hawker Sea Fury, was the first airplane to cross the finish line in the final Gold Race. But a pylon cut on the last lap cost Anderson the win. The resulting 16-second penalty allowed Steve Hinton, piloting the *Super Corsair,* to win the Unlimited Championship in 1985.

The 1986 National Championship Air Races began on a bad

note for the *Rare Bear* crew. John Penney was again at the controls when an engine failure forced *Rare Bear* down with an emergency situation. Fortunately, a stock engine was located and installed in time for Penney to qualify at a slow, but nevertheless respectable, 402.171 mph. In spite of having only a stock engine, Penney went on to place second in Heat 1-A and Heat 2-B, and win Heat 3-B. His performance was good enough to get into the final Gold Race on Sunday. Penney made the best of his stock motor, but *Rare Bear* did not have enough horsepower to really challenge the R-4360-powered Sea Furies piloted by Rick Brickert flying *Dreadnought* and Lloyd Hamilton piloting *Furias*.

Air racing is not only the "fastest motor sport in the world," but it is also one of the more expensive sports. It takes a great deal of money to keep a racer in top condition every year, and many of the owners who bring their airplanes to Reno rely heavily on sponsorship money to defray the total cost of competition. In 1987, Shelton partnered with Jack DeBoer's Wichita

Air Service. The new influx of money helped Shelton bring *Rare Bear* back to top racing form.

Only two pilots had qualified at over 450 mph in the history of Reno Unlimited Air Racing. Skip Holm was the first to break the 450-mph barrier in 1981 (450.085), and Rick Brickert followed him in 1986 (452.737 mph). In 1987, history was made as all three top qualifiers flew faster than 450 mph. Bill "Tiger" Destefani took the top slot and set a new qualifying record with a speed of 466.674 mph. Tiger was followed by Steven Hinton (464.649 mph) who was flying *Tsunami*, the purpose-built racer designed by Bruce Boland and built by John Sandberg, and of course Lyle Shelton's newly energized *Rare Bear* at 452.490 mph.

It appeared that the top qualifiers had the potential to really give race fans something to look forward to, but 1987 was not to be a winning year for Lyle Shelton or Steve Hinton. *Tsunami* had to leave Heat 3-A early. While it was landing the main gear collapsed, putting Hinton and his crew on the sidelines for Sunday's Gold Race. *Rare Bear* made it to the finals, but a problem with the aircraft's ignition system forced Shelton to declare a mayday in the

second lap of the Gold Race. Destefani and his P-51 *Strega* set a new course record of 452.559 mph, in addition to winning the 1987 Unlimited National Championship.

1988–1992: SHELTON AND *RARE BEAR* DOMINATE RENO RACING

Lyle Shelton began a four-year dominance of the Unlimited Class of air racing by first winning the Gold Race at the 1988 Wings of Victory Air Races. The event was held at Hamilton Field north of San Francisco, California, on May 6-8, 1988. The race course, which extended into San Francisco Bay, measured 9.091 miles. Some of the course markers were on boats that were disturbed by a storm a few days before qualifying. As a result, the actual lap distance varied, without question, from the original measurements. The incorrect lap distance resulted in slower calculated speeds. Shelton was the top qualifier at 411.095 mph and in the Gold Race was matched up against Tiger Destefani in *Strega*. For the better part of eight laps (72.728 miles) Shelton and Destefani challenged each other for the lead, and when the race concluded the records showed respective speeds of

412.492 mph and 412.284 mph, with *Rare Bear* crossing the finish line first. Shelton's 0.208-mph margin of victory was one of the closest race finishes in recent memory.

Three months later, Shelton was ready to extend his winning streak by capturing the Gold at Reno. He again established a new qualifying record at 474.622 mph. Shelton's strategy was to save the engine in the heat races, and then pour on the power in the Gold Race, which he won for the third time in his career with a course record of 456.821mph.

After Reno, Shelton and his crew began to look for new ways to make *Rare Bear* faster. The aerodynamics of the aircraft had already been worked over many times, so the focus was directed toward the engine and propeller setup. Crewmember and retired Lockheed engineer Carl Friend came up with the idea of using Hamilton Standard 7121A-type blades, which were originally installed on the Lockheed P-3 Orion. Friend figured that the 13-foot Aeroproducts H20-162 propeller was likely losing much of its efficiency at speeds over 450 mph due to airflow compressibility. One possible solution to this problem was to install a higher-speed propeller that

Butch Morris piloted F8F-2 N618F, BuNo 121748, Race Number 7, to a ninth place finish at the California 1,000 air race at Mojave in 1971. (William T. Larkins)

John Herlihy acquired N7827C from Tom Matthews and renamed the aircraft Sweet P. *Walt Ohlrich and Sandy Falconer had previously raced this aircraft. (Gerry Liang)*

Shelton had control problems with Rare Bear *at the start of the Bakersfield Gold Race. It took a few laps but he finally figured out how to control the Bear with a combination of trim and rudder.* (Neal Nurmi)

Thomason Aircraft Corporation sponsored Rare Bear *in 1992. The new green and white paint scheme was an attractive departure from the brown and white version that adorned the racer between 1988 and 1991.* (Neal Nurmi)

had lower blade section drag. This would allow the engine to run at reduced power while generating the same amount of thrust. Early in 1989 blades were purchased and fitted to a 33E60 Hamilton Standard propeller hub that was used on Lockheed's 1649 Super Constellation. The new airscrew was assembled by California Propeller Co., and first installed on the aircraft in August 1989. Problems with the new design during flight test led Shelton to delay its introduction to the air racing world, so *Rare Bear* reverted back to basically the same power plant and propeller system that had brought the team victory in 1988.

Late in August 1989, Shelton also made good on his attempt to break the world's speed record for an unlimited-weight, piston-engine aircraft. Plans to accomplish this feat had been made months before Shelton and his followers descended on Las Vegas, New Mexico. *Rare Bear* made several passes over the three-kilometer course on August 21, 1989. The average speed of the flights was 528.329 mph, which shattered the previous record of

499.04 mph, set by Steven Hinton in RB-51 *Red Baron* in 1979.

Not having the new propeller did not seem to affect *Rare Bear's* performance in 1989. Shelton was again the top qualifier at 467.378 mph, and easily won Heat 2-A, with an average speed of 443.331 mph, by outdistancing Rick Brickert in *Dreadnought*. Heat 3-A was a different matter altogether, and in many ways it was a repeat of what had happened at Hamilton Field three months before. This time Shelton was again pitted against Tiger Destefani's *Strega*. The finish of Heat 3-A was not as close as it was at Hamilton Field, but the end results were the same, with Shelton flying 1.44 mph faster that Destefani.

The 1989 Reno Gold Race was another classic battle between the *Rare Bear* and *Strega*. Shelton took the lead from the start as all of the racers came down the chute. At the end of the fourth lap *Rare Bear* and *Strega* were almost side-by-side as they began to separate from the rest of the pack. Destefani then passed Shelton and kept the lead for a short time. Shelton then engaged his nitrous

oxide injection system and retook the lead as the yellow smoke bellowed from *Rare Bear's* exhaust pipes. As the two leaders approached lap six, they began to lap the slower competitors. Then suddenly the word "mayday" was transmitted over the radio. It was Tiger Destefani, who was making the call as he departed the course with a hot-running engine. At that point all Shelton had to do to win the Gold in 1989 was maintain his lead on Rick Brickert and *Dreadnought*.

Rare Bear's new propeller development program and the subsequent test flights kept it out of both the 1990 Texas Air Races and the Colorado National Air Races, but the airplane was ready in time for Reno. Modifications made to the racer's propulsion system were all the talk in the pit area as spectators and race pilots alike passed by the ominous looking bird. Shelton's competition for the Gold was not standing still either. His chief rival, Bill Destefani, was back and faster than ever. Destefani put the power to his Mustang and qualified it at 470.246 mph, which was 1.877 mph

faster than *Rare Bear*. Skip Holm came in third at 465.187 mph. Holm had taken over the piloting duties for the *Tsunami* racing team after Steve Hinton was injured in an accident while stunt flying for a movie.

The Unlimited Heat Races in 1990 were all very competitive events. Shelton won both Heat 2-A and Heat 3-C but at times was hard pressed by both Destefani and Holm. In the Championship Race Shelton's Bearcat leaped out in front at the start but was overtaken by Holm and *Tsunami* on the backside of the course. All three racers— *Tsunami*, *Rare Bear*, and *Strega*—were line abreast as they passed the home pylon at the conclusion of the pace lap. Each of the top competitors would lead the race for some part of the third lap before Shelton finally began to slowly pull away from Holm and Destefani during the fourth lap. In lap five, Holm moved *Tsunami* above the wake of *Rare Bear*, but the maneuver was too little, too late. Three circuits later Shelton captured his third consecutive Unlimited Gold Championship trophy, with a new record of 468.620 mph.

Reno 1991 produced what is considered to be one of the most competitive and the fastest Gold competitions in Unlimited racing history. Shelton and his crew had *Rare Bare* running in fine order and again set a new course qualifying record at 475.899. Skip Holm had also returned to Stead Field flying John Sandberg's *Tsunami*. On the last day of qualifying Holm flew his racer around the course at better than 477 mph, but the timer got confused and officially clocked Holm on the wrong lap. Holm's 456.908-mph lap gave him the second position, and Tiger Destefani was the third fastest with an average speed of 449.840 mph.

The top qualifiers were exempt from participating in Thursday's heats; however, all three were ready for Heat 2-A on Friday. Tiger Destefani easily won the preliminary match by outdistancing both John Penney, who was giving Shelton a breather, and Skip Holm. The following day Shelton was again in control of *Rare Bear* for Heat 3-A. Destefani yet again averaged 461 mph, but Shelton was faster at 465.385 mph.

The outcome of the 1991 Reno Unlimited Gold Race was never really in doubt, as *Rare Bear* jumped ahead of the other racers, and Shelton never looked back. Trailing slightly behind throughout the eight laps around the 9.128-mile course were *Strega* and *Tsunami*. The performance of Shelton, Destefani, and Holm that day left no question in the minds of every race fan that these three great race pilots were giving it all they had. It was truly an amazing sight to see three highly tuned racers fly a complete race without holding back. When the checkered flag finally dropped, all three of the top qualifiers had broken Shelton's 1990 record. *Rare Bear* had an average speed of 481.618 mph and one lap was clocked at more than 490 mph. Destefani's and Holm's efforts were no less impressive, as each averaged more than 478 mph. Shelton's four-year win streak is only surpassed by Darryl Greenamyer's 1965–1969 run, and Shelton was very much looking forward to tying Greenamyer's record in 1992.

Sadly, this was the last race for *Tsunami*. Owner John Sandberg was ferrying the purpose-built racer back to Minneapolis when he attempted to land at Pierre, South Dakota, for fuel. While approaching the field the racer suddenly rolled into the ground, killing Sandberg. It was later determined that only one flap

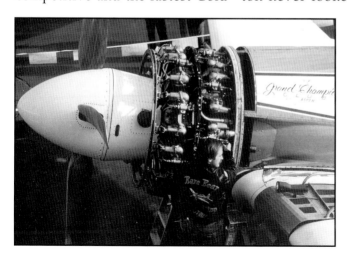

These photos show the after body fairing that was adapted to Rare Bear's *spinner. This device helps eliminate the mismatch that exists between the engine and the propeller. It also helps direct cooling air to the engine's cylinders. (Neal Nurmi)*

had extended when Sandberg approached the field and he was too low to recover the aircraft from its violent maneuver.

In 1992, Lyle Shelton and the *Rare Bear* crew were poised to win their fifth consecutive Unlimited Gold Championship by setting a new qualifying speed of 482.891 mph. His closest competitor was Tiger Destefani, but *Strega's* qualifying speed (452.130 mph) was almost 30 mph slower than *Rare Bear's*. However, it was not to be. *Rare Bear's* engine began running rough while John Penney was out practicing over the course on the last day for qualifying. The cause was traced to a burnt piston. The crew worked long hours and managed to keep the ailing airplane in the race. It is interesting to note that four additional racers experienced engine failures during the Silver Heat Race the following day. Losing an engine is one of the risks of racing; however, this time, there was a very strange coincidence. That is, all five of the stricken airplanes had been fueled at about the same time on Wednesday. Shelton recalled what caused the R-3350s to fail in 1992: "The Reno Air Race Association (RARA), without consulting the pilots, decided, in an attempt to save money, to use gas that was left over from 1991. The fuel was stored in an old Air Force underground tank, and all the gums (viscous residues formed in gasoline, mainly by slow oxidation) had settled out of the old gasoline. RARA consulted Phillips Petroleum, who analyzed a sample and certified that the 1991 fuel was usable. So, RARA added approximately 5,000 gallons of fresh fuel on top of the old gas and stirred up all the old gums back into suspension from the bottom of the tank, and sold the gas to the race participants. Pete Law, along with another respected engineer, did an extensive study and wrote a full report, which concluded that those gums in the old gas formed hotspots in our engines after running a few minutes. The hot spots caused uncontrollable ignition and all of the R-3350s on the field burned pistons. That's the reason why *Rare Bear* started running rough when John Penny was on the course that day. After flying about 25 minutes, enough gum collected on the pistons to form hot spots. All the P-51s were running rough as well, but they did not fail their engines the way we did. A lawsuit was filed against RARA, which was eventually settled out of court."

On Friday, Shelton started Heat 2-A, but left the course after only completing the first lap. Shelton wanted to get credit for the start and, at the same time, save his less than perfect engine for Saturday and Sunday. The following day Shelton coaxed 449.984 mph out of his R-3350 engine during Heat 3-A. Tiger Destefani won the heat, but Shelton's effort sent a clear message that the *Bear* would certainly show up for the Gold on Sunday.

The first four laps of the 1992 Unlimited Gold Race surpassed the week's long buildup, pitting *Strega* against the *Bear*. *Strega* took the early lead, but could not shake Shelton, who was close behind. In the fifth lap both aircraft were dead even, when *Rare Bear's* engine failed. As Shelton pulled off the course he shouted "Go Tiger Go!" over the radio. He then made an emergency

During the Reno 1990 Unlimited Gold Race, Shelton was pursued closely by Skip Holm in Tsunami, *Bill "Tiger" Destefani in* Strega, *Rick Brickert in* Dreadnought, *and John Maloney in the* Super Corsair. *Shelton won the race, posting a speed of 468.620 mph. An elated Shelton emerged from the cockpit cheering his third Reno victory. He then sprayed his crew and his sponsor, Jack DeBoar, on Shelton's left, with champagne. (Nicholas A. Veronico)*

landing and had to ground loop his Bearcat as the fast-moving racer approached the end of the runway. Fortunately, Shelton was safe and no additional damage was done to his racer. Tiger Destefani went on to win the Gold.

1993–2000
TURMOIL FOR *RARE BEAR*

The balance of the 1990s was a bittersweet period for Lyle Shelton. The broken engine kept *Rare Bear* out of competition in 1993, and in 1994 Shelton experienced some trouble getting the FAA to reinstate his medical certification. Back-up pilot John Penney filled in while Shelton was grounded. Penney won both the Phoenix 500 Gold competition, and the 1994 Reno Super Gold Shootout. The following year Penney repeated as Gold Champion at Phoenix, but came in second to Tiger Destefani for the Reno Gold.

Reno 1996 was on track to be a banner year for air racing. David Price, leader of the Museum of Flying in Santa Monica, California, came to Reno with veteran racer *Dago Red* and he was determined to take the championship away from perennial winners *Rare Bear* and *Strega*. In the off-season, Bruce Lockwood, director of the museum's air racing program, contracted with master engine builder Dwight Thorn for a Rolls-Royce Merlin similar to the type that was used by the *Strega* team. The results of the contract, along with all the other preparations made by Lockwood and Price, became evident when *Dago Red* qualified at 490.826 mph. This was not only a record, but it was the fastest official speed ever recorded for a Mustang. Not to be out done, John Penney also had a fast machine in 1996. *Rare Bear* was running better than ever, so Penney

Since 1977 Conquest 1 *has been on display at the National Air & Space Museum restoration facility in Silver Hill, Maryland. In the near future, it will be moved to the Museum's new facility, under construction near Dulles Airport in northern Virginia.* (David Schwartz)

just went out on the course and bested Price's speed by posting a 491.266 mph lap. Tiger Destefani qualified third at 465.516 mph with an experimental propeller called the "Tiger Claw."

The top three qualifiers did not compete in Thursday's competitions, and bad weather moved into Reno overnight, so the races scheduled on Friday were canceled. Penney was concerned that *Rare Bear* was not running as well as his qualified speed indicated. He figured that they were down on horsepower, but the crew could not isolate the cause.

Dago Red jumped out in front of *Strega* and *Rare Bear* in Heat 2-A as the airplanes headed down the chute. Before the race, Destefani had replaced the disappointing "Tiger Claw" airscrew with his standard racing propeller, and *Strega* appeared to have the power to keep pace with *Dago Red*. John Penney was also flying very fast, but was

not keeping up with the two front-runners. Later in the race *Rare Bear's* engine seemed to hesitate slightly, just as Penney passed the home pylon. Price, Destefani, and Penney finished the competition one, two, and three with respective speeds of 479.929, 477.632, and 473.160 mph.

As the Gold Race approached, fans braced themselves for possibly the fastest contest in Reno history. Price took the lead at the start of the Gold Race while *Strega* and *Rare Bear* battled for who would be the first to pass *Dago Red*. Then John Penney pulled out of the race with his engine smoking. Apparently *Rare Bear's* engine cough in Saturday's race resulted in hidden cylinder damage that did not become totally acute until the Unlimited Gold Race. Price continued to lead Destefani as the two Dwight Thorn-powered Mustangs screamed around the pylons. For reasons that were unknown at the time, Destefani

Rare Bear set yet another record in the Reno qualifying rounds in 1996. His 491.266 mph was just slightly ahead of David Price's speed of 490.826 mph. (A. Kevin Grantham)

The words on this shirt accurately describe the racer known as Rare Bear. (Neal Nurmi)

began to fall back behind Price toward the end of lap five. Price did not let up and three laps later took the checkered flag to win what appeared to be his first championship. Shortly thereafter, the air race announcer broadcast that *Dago Red* had cut pylon six during lap

A jubilant John Penney poses with the 1994 Unlimited Super Gold Shootout trophy. Penney flew the race at 424.407 mph. (Chuck Aro)

five. The 16-second penalty dropped Price's speed to 460.557 mph, which made Tiger Destefani the winner of the 1996 Reno Unlimited Championship Gold Race.

Lyle Shelton finally got his medical certification approved by the FAA and was back in *Rare Bear's* cockpit for Reno 1997. Shelton qualified in second position behind Tiger Destefani, but *Rare Bear's* engine was still not running as well as it had in the past. Both Heat 2-A and Heat 3-A were more or less a repeat of the qualifying round, with *Strega* finishing ahead of the *Bear*. One had to wonder if Shelton's radial engine could produce enough horsepower to overcome *Strega* and win the gold for a seventh time. The answer was forthcoming on Sunday. Shelton flew a fine race in spite of engine problems that began in lap three when he climbed to 500 feet for a safety margin and cut a pylon, as he continued to race. Rare Bear's engine gradually lost power due to an ignition problem and later experienced an exhaust system failure. Destefani easily won the 1997 Gold with *Rare Bear* finishing in third place.

The lack of money to fix *Rare Bear's* engine and exhaust problems kept Shelton from competing in 1998. The high point, at least from a Bearcat point of view, of Reno 1998 was the entry of three stock Grumman F8Fs, owned by the Museum of Flying, veteran race pilot Howard Pardue, and former Apollo astronaut Bill Anders. All three of the Bearcats were featured in the final Bronze Race, and the trio finished one, two, and three, with Howard Pardue's rare XF8F-1 winning the competition.

In 1999, *Rare Bear* returned to Reno with Matt Jackson joining Shelton's team as pilot and, according to Shelton, as "the payer of all racing expenses and any subsequent repairs." Jackson was the first to qualify *Rare Bear* in 1999 at approximately 462 mph by using all the nitrous oxide-boosted horsepower that was available. Later in the day veteran *Bear* pilot John Penny officially qualified Race Number 77 at 468.780 mph without the benefit of nitrous oxide. That was approximately 10 mph slower than the two top qualifiers *Strega* and *Dago Red*. During Penney's run, an exhaust clamp

Lyle Shelton was back in Rare Bear's *cockpit in 1997 after a long hiatus. Shelton showed that he still knew how to fly the fast bird by qualifying second at 461.508 mph. (A. Kevin Grantham)*

Former Apollo 8 astronaut William A. Anders brought N800H back to Reno as Wampus Cat *in 1998. The former* Tonopah Queen *of 1960s racing fame is now competitive in the Unlimited Bronze and Silver classes. (Shawn Aro)*

broke, and the escaping hot gases damaged one of the cylinder heads, but there was plenty of time to get the Bearcat ready for Friday's contest.

Matt Jackson suffered a bird strike shortly after the start of Heat 2-A. The race was shaping up to be a competitive affair when Jackson suddenly pulled off the course. On the ground, it appeared that the hungry *Bear* had ingested the ill-fated bird, but apparently the bird strike caused no engine damage.

Saturday, September 18, 1999, marked a dark day for Unlimited Air Racing, as veteran race pilot Gary Levitz was lost in a fatal crash. Levitz

and builder Bill Rogers had originally teamed up in 1997 to bring a Rolls-Royce Griffon-powered Mustang to Reno. The hybrid racer sported Lear Jet wings and numerous other improvements (see *RaceplaneTech Series, Vol. I: Griffon-Powered Racing Mustangs*). The aircraft sadly suffered a structural failure as Levitz was setting up his turn on pylon 2. Jackson continued to fly until the fifth lap, when he was forced to leave the race with engine difficulties.

No Bearcats have raced since 1999. Howard Pardue's rare XF8F-1 was damaged in an accident at Oshkosh in 2000, and the lack of

money for a new engine has kept Shelton and his crew out of racing, as well. It looked as though *Rare Bear* might be back in 2001 but financing fell through during the summer. According to Shelton, Matt Jackson failed to provide a race-ready engine in accordance with the legal agreement he had signed prior to Reno 1999, and that is what kept the *Bear* from competing in 2000. The races were canceled as a result of the September 11 terrorist attack in New York City and Washington, D.C. Hopefully the future will bring good fortune back to those who fly *The Fastest Cats in the World.*

Rare Bear, minus its engine, briefly appeared on the ramp during Reno 2000. One can only hope that this great racer will once again fly the pylons. (A. Kevin Grantham)

One of the greatest rivalries in air racing history is that between the Merlin-powered Strega *and the R-3350-powered* Rare Bear. *(Chuck Aro)*

BEARCAT RACERS

Race	Pilot	Name	Reg. No.	Type	BuNo.	Notes
1	Darryl Greenamyer	*Conquest I*	N1111L	F8F-2	121646	
4	Jack Sliker	*Escape II*	N7701C	F8F-2	122708	
7	Thomas Morris		N618F	F8F-2	121748	
7	Gunther Balz		N9G	F8F-1	90454	(also raced as Race No. 1)
8	Harold Beal		N800H	F8F-2	121752	
10	Thomas P. Matthews	*Tom's Cat*	N7827C	F8F-2	121752	
	Walt Olrich	*Miss Priss*				
	Sandy Falconer					(1966)
	John Herlihy	*Sweet P*				
	Whittington Brothers	*Precious Bear*				
	Whittington Brothers	*Bearcat Bill*				
11	Chuck Klusmann		N148F	F8F-2P	121787	
	John Church					
14	Howard Pardue		NL14HP	XF8F-1	90446	
24	Bud Fountain	*Hawke Dusters*	N148F	F8F-2	121787	(also raced as Race No. 99)
41	Mike Smith	*Lois Jean*	N9885C	F8F-2	121751	
44	Ron Reynolds/Mike Geren		N5005	F8F-2	121731	(also raced as Race Nos. 14, 44, 66)
77	Lyle Shelton	*Rare Bear*	N777L	F8F-2	122619	(also raced as Race No. 70)
80	Mira Slovak	*Smirnoff*	N9885C	F8F-2	121751	
98	John Gury		N198F	F8F-2	122637	(also raced as Race Nos. 11 and 99)
99	Bob Kucera		N212KA	F8F-2	121528	
106	William A. Anders	*Wampus Cat*	N800H	F8F-2	121752	
201	David G. Price/Alan Preston		N41089	F8F-1	95255	

BEARCAT B RACERS

Race #: 1   **Type:** Grumman F8F-2 Bearcat   **BuNo:** 121646   **N#:** N1111L

Year	Event	Race	Pilot	Aircraft's Name	MPH	Finish
1964	Reno NCAR	Qualification	D. Greenamyer		359.51	2nd
1964	Reno NCAR	Heat 2	D. Greenamyer		356.58	Disqualified
1964	Reno NCAR	Heat 4	D. Greenamyer		————	Did Not Start
1964	Reno NCAR	Championship	D. Greenamyer		351.88	Disqualified
1965	Reno NCAR	Qualification	D. Greenamyer		369.70	1st
1965	Reno NCAR	Heat 1	D. Greenamyer		364.60	2nd
1965	Reno NCAR	Heat 3	D. Greenamyer		368.81	1st
1965	Reno NCAR	Championship	D. Greenamyer		375.10	1st
1965	Las Vegas IAR	Qualification	D. Greenamyer		423.40	1st
1965	Las Vegas IAR	Heat 1-A	D. Greenamyer		385.57	1 st
1965	Las Vegas IAR	Heat 2-A	D. Greenamyer		376.0	1 st
1965	Las Vegas IAR	Championship	D. Greenamyer		————	Out 9th lap
1966	Los Angeles NAR	Qualification	D. Greenamyer		————	Did Not Qualify
1966	Reno NCAR	Qualification	D. Greenamyer	Smirnoff	409.972	1st
1966	Reno NCAR	Heat 1	D. Greenamyer	Smirnoff	365.22	1st
1966	Reno NCAR	Championship	D. Greenamyer	Smirnoff	396.221	1st
1967	Reno NCAR	Qualification	D. Greenamyer	Smirnoff	408.814	1st
1967	Reno NCAR	Championship	D. Greenamyer	Smirnoff	392.621	1st
1968	Reno NCAR	Qualification	D. Greenamyer	Greenamyer Bearcat		
1968	Reno NCAR	Heat 1-B	D. Greenamyer	Greenamyer Bearcat	374.388	3rd
1968	Reno NCAR	Championship	D. Greenamyer	Greenamyer Bearcat	388.654	1st
1969	Reno NCAR	Qualification	D. Greenamyer	Conquest I	414.63	1st
1969	Reno NCAR	Heat 1	D. Greenamyer	Conquest I	351.93	1st
1969	Reno NCAR	Championship	D. Greenamyer	Conquest I	412.631	1st, New Record
1970	Reno NCAR	Qualification	D. Greenamyer	Conquest I	378.245	2nd
1970	Reno NCAR	Heat 2	D. Greenamyer	Conquest I	351.522	3rd
1970	Reno NCAR	Championship	D. Greenamyer	Conquest I	297.063	6th
1971	Reno NCAR	Qualification	D. Greenamyer	Conquest I	405.984	4th
1971	Reno NCAR	Heat 1-B	D. Greenamyer	Conquest I	396.627	2nd
1971	Reno NCAR	Championship	D. Greenamyer	Conquest I	413.987	1st, New Race Record
1972	Reno NCAR	Qualification	R. Laidley	Conquest I	411.189	1st
1972	Reno NCAR	Heat 1	R. Laidley	Conquest I	403.507	1st
1972	Reno NCAR	Championship	R. Laidley	Conquest I		Disqualified for flying too low
1975	California NAR	Qualification	D. Greenamyer	American Jet	418.49	1st
1975	California NAR	Championship	D. Greenamyer	American Jet	410.68	3rd
1975	Reno NAR	Qualification	D. Greenamyer	American Jet	435.556	1s, New Record
1975	Reno NAR	Championship	D. Greenamyer	American Jet		Did Not Start

Race #: 4   **Type:** Grumman F8F-1 Bearcat   **BuNo:** 122708   **N#:** N7707C

Year	Event	Heat/Race	Pilot	Aircraft's Name	MPH	Finish
1973	Great Miami Air Race	Qualification	Jack Sliker	Escape II	383.562	1st
1973	Great Miami Air Race	Heat 1	Jack Sliker	Escape II	338.929	1st
1973	Great Miami Air Race	Heat 1-A	Jack Sliker	Escape II	347.782	2nd
1973	Great Miami Air Race	Turner Speed Classic	Jack Sliker	Escape II	366.470	2nd
1973	Reno NCAR	Qualification	Jack Sliker	Escape II	407.390	5th
1973	Reno NCAR	Heat 1	Jack Sliker	Escape II	390.626	3rd
1973	Reno NCAR	Championship	Jack Sliker	Escape II	387.598	4th
1974	Reno NCAR	Qualification	Jack Sliker	Escape II	396.000	6th
1974	Reno NCAR	Heat 2	Jack Sliker	Escape II		6th, out lap 1
1974	Reno NCAR	Consolation	Jack Sliker	Escape II	374.813	2nd
1974	Reno NCAR	Consolation	Jack Sliker	Escape II	373.520	1st
1974	California NAR	Qualifications	Jack Sliker	Escape II	357.686	5th
1974	California NAR	Heat	Jack Sliker	Escape II	315.020	1st
1974	California NAR	Silver	Jack Sliker	Escape II		Did Not Finish
1974	California NAR	Championship	Jack Sliker	Escape II	369.504	4th
1975	California NAR	Qualifications	Jack Sliker	Escape II	397.04	5th
1975	California NAR	Silver	Jack Sliker	Escape II	374.08	1st
1975	California NAR	Championship	Jack Sliker	Escape II	383.94	4th
1975	Reno NAR	Qualifications	Jack Sliker	Escape II	393.311	8th
1975	Reno NAR	Consolidation	Jack Sliker	Escape II	387.196	1st
1975	Reno NAR	Championship	Jack Sliker	Escape II	381.973	3rd

Race #: 7   **Type:** Grumman F8F-1 Bearcat   **BuNo:** 90454   **N#:** N9G

Year	Event	Heat/Race	Pilot	Aircraft's Name	MPH	Finish
1966	Reno NAR	Heat 2	Chuck Klusman		355.36	1st
1966	Reno NAR	Consolation	Chuck Klusman		342.74	4th
1967	Harold's Club Transcontinental Trophy Dash		John Church			Did Not Start
1967	Reno NAR	Qualification	John Church		332.690	9th

Year	Event	Race	Pilot	Aircraft's Name	MPH	Finish
1967	Reno NAR	Consolation	John Church		336.167	2nd
1968	Harold's Club Transcontinental Trophy Dash		Gunther Balz			Did Not Start
1969	Harold's Club Transcontinental Trophy Dash		Gunther Balz		265.460	7th
1969	Reno NCAR	Qualification	Gunther Balz	Roto Finish	348.92	7th
1969	Reno NCAR	Heat 1	Gunther Balz	Roto Finish	345.76	2nd
1969	Reno NAR	Consolation	Gunther Baltz	Roto Finish	305.24	6th
1969	Reno NAR	Championship	Gunther Baltz	Roto Finish	318.288	6th
1970	Harold's Club Transcontinental Trophy Dash		Gunther Baltz	Roto Finish	273.453	2nd
1970	Reno NCAR	Qualification	Gunther Baltz	Roto Finish	361.702	8th
1970	Reno NCAR	Heat 2	Gunther Baltz	Roto Finish	353.757	2nd
1970	Reno NCAR	Championship	Gunther Baltz	Roto Finish	334.426	5th
1970	California 1000	Qualification	Gunther Baltz	Roto Finish	302.09	8th
1970	California 1000	Race	Gunther Baltz	Roto Finish		11th (57 laps)
1971	NAR, Cape May, New Jersey	Qualification	Gunther Baltz	Roto Finish	344.33	2nd, cut pylon
1971	NAR, Cape May, New Jersey	Heat 1-A	Gunther Baltz	Roto Finish	306.88	1st
1971	NAR, Cape May, New Jersey	Heat 2-B	Gunther Baltz	Roto Finish	309.43	4th, cut pylon
1971	NAR, Cape May, New Jersey	Consolation	Gunther Baltz	Roto Finish	341.57	4th
1971	NAR, Cape May, New Jersey	Championship	Gunther Baltz	Roto Finish	332.40	3rd

Race #: 7 **Type:** Grumman F8F-2 Bearcat **BuNo:** 121748 **N#:** N618F

Year	Event	Race	Pilot	Aircraft's Name	MPH	Finish
1971	California 1000 Air Race	1000 miles	Butch Morris		290.95, 35 laps	9th

Race #: 10 (1964), 8 (1972), 106 (1998) **Type:** Grumman F8F-2 Bearcat **BuNo:** 121752 **N#:** N7827C (1964), N800H (1972)

Year	Event	Heat/Race	Pilot	Aircraft's Name	MPH	Finish
1964	Reno NCAR	Qualification	Walter Ohlrich		351.29	4th
1964	Reno NCAR	Heat 1	Walter Ohlrich		339.55	2nd
1964	Reno NCAR	Heat 3	Walter Ohlrich		337.41	3rd
1964	Reno NCAR	Championship	Walter Ohlrich		343.43	5th
1965	Reno NCAR	Qualification	Walter Ohlrich	Tonopah Queen	325.79	6th
1965	Reno NCAR	Heat 2	Walter Ohlrich	Tonopah Queen	335.70	4th
1965	Reno NCAR	Heat 3	Walter Ohlrich	Tonopah Queen	331.42	4th
1965	Reno NCAR	Championship	Walter Ohlrich	Tonopah Queen	333.22	5th
1965	Las Vegas IAR	Qualification	Walter Ohlrich	Tonopah Queen	329.35	9th
1965	Las Vegas IAR	Heat 1-A	Walter Ohlrich	Tonopah Queen	322.11	4th
1965	Las Vegas IAR	Heat 2-B	Walter Ohlrich	Tonopah Queen	316.5	2nd
1965	Las Vegas IAR	Championship	Walter Ohlrich	Tonopah Queen	319.37	4th
1966	Los Angeles NAR	Qualification	Walter Ohlrich	Tonopah Queen	———	Not Recorded
1966	Los Angeles NAR	Heat 1	Walter Ohlrich	Tonopah Queen	338.36	5th
1966	Los Angeles NAR	Heat 2	Walter Ohlrich	Tonopah Queen	339.38	3rd
1966	Los Angeles NAR	Championship	Walter Ohlrich	Tonopah Queen	362.65	4th
1966	Reno NCAR	Qualification	Sandy Falconer	Tom's Cat	333.46	9th
1966	Reno NCAR	Heat 2	Sandy Falconer	Tom's Cat	324.85	4th
1966	Reno NCAR	Consolation	Sandy Falconer	Tom's Cat	351.05	3rd
1967	Reno NCAR	Qualification	Walter Ohlrich	Tom's Cat	333.841	8th
1967	Reno NCAR	Consolation	Walter Ohlrich	Tom's Cat	332.881	3rd
1968	Harold's Club Transcontinental Trophy Dash		Walter Ohlrich	Tom's Cat		Did Not Start
1968	Reno NCAR	Qualification	Walter Ohlrich	Miss Priss		
1968	Reno NCAR	Heat 1-A	Walter Ohlrich	Miss Priss	323.410	3rd
1968	Reno NCAR	Championship	Walter Ohlrich	Miss Priss	344.304	4th
1969	Harold's Club Transcontinental Trophy Dash		Walter Ohlrich	Miss Priss	254.990	8th
1969	Reno NAR	Qualification	Walter Ohlrich	Miss Priss	341.90	9th
1969	Reno NAR	Heat 2	Walter Ohlrich	Miss Priss	338.57	5th
1969	Reno NAR	Consolation	Walter Ohlrich	Miss Priss	344.17	1st
1969	Reno NAR	Medallion	Walter Ohlrich	Miss Priss	318.09	2nd
1971	Reno NCAR	Qualification	Walter Ohlrich	Miss Priss	358.537	10th
1971	Reno NCAR	Heat 1-B	Walter Ohlrich	Miss Priss	378.270	4th
1971	Reno NCAR	Silver Consolation	Walter Ohlrich	Miss Priss	352.729	3rd
1972	Reno NCAR	Qualification	John Herlihy	Sweet P	332.203	14th
1972	Reno NCAR	Heat 2	John Herlihy	Sweet P	331.995	4th
1972	Reno NCAR	Consolation	John Herlihy	Sweet P	343.441	4th
1972	Reno NCAR	Medallion	John Herlihy	Sweet P	343.692	2nd
1973	Reno NCAR	Qualification	John Herlihy	Sweet P	400.909	6th
1973	Reno NCAR	Heat 2	John Herlihy	Sweet P		6th, out 1st lap
1973	Reno NCAR	Consolation	John Herlihy	Sweet P		7th, out 4th lap
1977	Reno NCAR	Qualification	Don Whittington	Precious Bear	350.696	13th
1977	Reno NCAR	Heat 1A	Don Whittington	Precious Bear	307.921	5th
1977	Reno NCAR	Consolation	Don Whittington	Precious Bear	330.750	4th
1979	Miami, International AR	Qualification	Bill Whittington	Advance Machine Special	303.980	16th
1979	Miami, International AR	Medallion Heat 1	Bill Whittington	Advance Machine Special	302.666	1st
1979	Miami, International AR	Silver Heat 2	Bill Whittington	Advance Machine Special	287.277	7th
1979	Miami, International AR	Medallion	Bill Whittington	Advance Machine Special	329.627	1st
1980	Reno NCAR	Qualification	Bill Whittington	Precious Bear	335.975	18th
1980	Reno NCAR	Bronze Heat 1	Bill Whittington	Precious Bear	326.392	3rd
1980	Reno NCAR	Bronze Heat 2	Bill Whittington	Precious Bear	320.636	5th
1980	Reno NCAR	Bronze	Bill Whittington	Precious Bear	344.666	1st
1981	Reno NCAR	Qualification	Bill Whittington	Bearcat Bill	333.395	20th
1981	Reno NCAR	Bronze Heat 1	Bill Whittington	Bearcat Bill	335.045	2nd
1981	Reno NCAR	Silver Heat 2	Bill Whittington	Bearcat Bill		Pulled out early
1988	Reno NCAR	Qualification	Bill Whittington			Did Not Qualify
1998	Reno NCAR	Qualification	Bill Anders	Wampus Cat	359.899	21st

Year	Event	Heat/Race	Pilot	Aircraft's Name	MPH	Finish
1998	Reno NCAR	Heat 1-C	Bill Anders	*Wampus Cat*	351.976	3rd
1998	Reno NCAR	Heat 2-C	Bill Anders	*Wampus Cat*	348.979	5th
1998	Reno NCAR	Heat 3-C	Bill Anders	*Wampus Cat*	338.954	7th
1998	Reno NCAR	Bronze	Bill Anders	*Wampus Cat*	364.391	2nd
1999	Reno NCAR	Qualification	Bill Anders	*Wampus Cat*	388.591	16th
1999	Reno NCAR	Heat 1-B	Bill Anders	*Wampus Cat*	378.771	2nd
1999	Reno NCAR	Heat 2-C	Bill Anders	*Wampus Cat*		Did Not Finish

Race #: 11 (1966), 99 (1969), 24 (1973) **Type:** *Grumman F8F-2 Bearcat* **BuNo:** 121787 **N#:** N148F

Year	Event	Heat/Race	Pilot	Aircraft's Name	MPH	Finish
1966	Reno NAR	Qualification	Chuck Klusman		357.33	7th
1966	Reno NAR	Heat 2	Chuck Klusman		355.36	1st
1966	Reno NAR	Consolation	Chuck Klusman		342.74	4th
1967	Reno NAR	Cross Country	John Church			Did Not Start
1967	Reno NAR	Qualification	John Church		332.690	9th
1967	Reno NAR	Consolation	John Church		336.167	2nd
1969	Reno NCAR	Qualification	Bud Fountain			Did Not Qualify
1973	Reno NCAR	Qualification	Bud Fountain	*Hawke Dusters*	378.947	10th
1973	Reno NCAR	Heat 2	Bud Fountain	*Hawke Dusters*	386.066	2nd
1973	Reno NCAR	Championship	Bud Fountain	*Hawke Dusters*		7th, out lap 5
1973	California Air Races	Qualification	Bud Fountain	*Hawke Dusters*	362.208	4th
1973	California Air Races	Heat 1-A	Bud Fountain	*Hawke Dusters*	356.306	3rd, crashed fatally after race

Race #: 14 **Type:** *Grumman XF8F-1* **BuNo:** 90446 **N#:** NL14HP

Year	Event	Heat/Race	Pilot	Aircraft's Name	Speed MPH	Finish
1983	Reno NCAR	Qualification	Howard Pardue		375.746	12th
1983	Reno NCAR	Silver Heat 1	Howard Pardue		337.017	7th
1983	Reno NCAR	Bronze Heat 2	Howard Pardue		360.209	5th
1983	Reno NCAR	Bronze	Howard Pardue			Out last lap
1984	Reno NCAR	Qualification	Howard Pardue		375.832	14th
1984	Reno NCAR	Heat 2	Howard Pardue		372.719	1st
1984	Reno NCAR	Heat 5	Howard Pardue		361.792	5th
1984	Reno NCAR	Heat 8	Howard Pardue		363.628	3rd
1984	Reno NCAR	Silver	Howard Pardue		348.671	4th, cut pylon 8 on lap 3
1985	Bakersfield NAR	Qualification	Howard Pardue		360.000	8th
1985	Bakersfield NAR	Silver Heat	Howard Pardue			Did Not Start
1985	Bakersfield NAR	Silver	Howard Pardue		352.704	1st
1985	Reno NAR	Qualification	Howard Pardue		369.167	18th
1985	Reno NAR	Heat 1-B	Howard Pardue		359.244	7th, Cut pylon 8 on Pace Lap
1985	Reno NAR	Heat 2-C	Howard Pardue		360.202	4th , cut pylon 1 on lap 2
1985	Reno NAR	Heat 3-C	Howard Pardue		359.087	1st
1985	Reno NAR	Silver	Howard Pardue		359.415	5th
1986	Reno NAR	Qualification	Howard Pardue		372.690	16th
1986	Reno NAR	Heat 1-B	Howard Pardue		369.010	3rd
1986	Reno NAR	Heat 2-C	Howard Pardue		368.614	1st
1986	Reno NAR	Heat 3-B	Howard Pardue			Disqualified
1986	Reno NAR	Silver	Howard Pardue		357.667	7th, 7 laps
1987	Reno NAR	Qualification	Howard Pardue		376.536	14th
1987	Reno NAR	Heat 1-B	Howard Pardue		370.286	2nd
1987	Reno NAR	Heat 2-B	Howard Pardue		369.784	6th
1987	Reno NAR	Heat 3-B	Howard Pardue		372.850	4th
1987	Reno NAR	Silver	Howard Pardue		366.366	3rd
1988	Wings of Victory Air Races	Qualification	Howard Pardue		352.969	9th
1988	Wings of Victory Air Races	Gold	Howard Pardue		348.245	2nd
1988	Reno NAR	Qualification	Howard Pardue		386.725	17th
1988	Reno NAR	Heat 1-B	Howard Pardue		367.021	3rd
1988	Reno NAR	Heat 2-C	Howard Pardue		387.239	3rd
1988	Reno NAR	Heat 3-C	Howard Pardue		383.833	4th
1988	Reno NAR	Silver	Howard Pardue		370.592	7th
1989	Reno NAR	Qualification	Howard Pardue		381.551	19th
1989	Reno NAR	Heat 1-B	Howard Pardue		348.965	4th
1989	Reno NAR	Heat 2-C	Howard Pardue		362.271	2nd
1989	Reno NAR	Heat 3-C	Howard Pardue			Out lap 2
1989	Reno NAR	Heat 3-B	Howard Pardue		357.022	5th
1989	Reno NAR	Silver	Howard Pardue		364.390	5th
1990	Texas Air Races	Qualification	Howard Pardue		337.178	9th
1990	Texas Air Races	Silver Heat	Howard Pardue		346.535	1st
1990	Texas Air Races	Silver	Howard Pardue		328.832	4th, cut one pylon
1990	Colorado NAR	Qualification	Howard Pardue		341.493	7th
1990	Texas Air Races	Silver Heat	Howard Pardue		343.829	4th
1990	Texas Air Races	Silver	Howard Pardue		362.202	2nd , cut pylon 1 on lap 1
1990	Reno NAR	Qualification	Howard Pardue		371.602	19th
1991	Reno NAR	Qualification	Howard Pardue		368.065	19th
1991	Reno NAR	Heat 1-B	Howard Pardue		364.877	4th
1991	Reno NAR	Heat 2-C	Howard Pardue		336.424	4th
1991	Reno NAR	Heat 3-C	Howard Pardue		354.977	3rd
1991	Reno NAR	Bronze	Howard Pardue		348.494	1st
1992	Denver Air Races	Qualification	Howard Pardue		331.200	8th
1992	Denver Air Races	Silver Heat	Howard Pardue		336.507	3rd
1992	Denver Air Races	Silver	Howard Pardue		348.336	1st
1992	Reno NAR	Qualification	Howard Pardue		381.792	15th
1992	Reno NAR	Heat 1-B	Howard Pardue		350.104	3rd

1992	Reno NAR	Heat 2-B	Howard Pardue		330.160	7th, 5 laps
1992	Reno NAR	Heat 3-B	Howard Pardue		344.869	6th
1992	Reno NAR	Silver	Howard Pardue		368.612	3rd
1993	Reno NAR	Qualification	Howard Pardue		361.664	16th
1993	Reno NAR	Heat 1-B	Howard Pardue		339.957	5th
1993	Reno NAR	Heat 2-C	Howard Pardue		351.973	3rd
1993	Reno NAR	Heat 3-B	Howard Pardue		369.181	3rd
1993	Reno NAR	Silver	Howard Pardue		380.009	3rd
1993	Kansas City Air Races	Qualification	Nelson Ezell		349.09	12th
1993	Kansas City Air Races	Heat 1	Howard Pardue		282.16	4th
1993	Kansas City Air Races	Heat 3	Nelson Ezell		337.25	4th, cut pylon 7 on lap 3
1993	Kansas City Air Races	Reserve	Howard Pardue		320.90	4th, cut pylons 3 & 7 on lap 1
1994	Phoenix 500 Air Races	Qualification	Howard Pardue		350.130	13th
1994	Phoenix 500 Air Races	Heat 1-B	Howard Pardue		353.826	5th
1994	Phoenix 500 Air Races	Heat 2-C	Howard Pardue		319.988	3rd
1994	Phoenix 500 Air Races	Silver	Howard Pardue		355.069	3rd, 7 laps
1994	Reno NAR	Qualification	Howard Pardue		369.472	12th
1994	Reno NAR	Heat 1-A	Howard Pardue		340.004	4th
1994	Reno NAR	Heat 2-B	Howard Pardue		353.989	4th
1994	Reno NAR	Heat 3-B	Howard Pardue		333.308	5th
1994	Reno NAR	Silver	Howard Pardue		352.437	3rd, cut pylon 1 on lap 1
1995	Phoenix 500 Air Races	Qualification	Howard Pardue		359.471	8th
1995	Phoenix 500 Air Races	Pro Heat 1-B	Howard Pardue		362.457	2nd
1995	Phoenix 500 Air Races	Pro Heat 2-B	Howard Pardue		365.524	2nd
1995	Reno NAR	Qualification	Howard Pardue		356.215	12th
1995	Reno NAR	Heat 1-B	Howard Pardue		350.455	3rd
1995	Reno NAR	Heat 2-B	Howard Pardue		350.964	2nd
1995	Reno NAR	Heat 3-B	Howard Pardue		347.564	3rd
1995	Reno NAR	Silver	Howard Pardue		361.134	2nd
1996	Reno NAR	Qualification	Howard Pardue		374.226	9th
1996	Reno NAR	Heat 1-A	Howard Pardue		362.994	7th
1996	Reno NAR	Heat 2-B	Howard Pardue		362.080	3rd
1996	Reno NAR	Silver	Howard Pardue		374.778	2nd
1997	Reno NAR	Qualification	Howard Pardue		374.751	14th
1997	Reno NAR	Heat 1-B	Howard Pardue		361.355	4th
1997	Reno NAR	Heat 2-B	Howard Pardue		371.027	4th
1997	Reno NAR	Heat 3-B	Howard Pardue		367.094	8th
1997	Reno NAR	Bronze	Howard Pardue		367.412	2nd
1998	Reno NAR	Qualification	Howard Pardue		369.693	18th
1998	Reno NAR	Heat 1-C	Howard Pardue		365.273	1st
1998	Reno NAR	Heat 2-C	Howard Pardue		349.246	4th
1998	Reno NAR	Heat 3-C	Howard Pardue		356.774	4th, cut pylon 3 on pace lap
1998	Reno NAR	Bronze	Howard Pardue		366.569	1st

Race #: 44 (1970), 66 (1970)   Type: Grumman F8F-2 Bearcat   BuNo: 121731   N#: N5005

Year	Event	Heat/Race	Pilot	Aircraft's Name	Speed MPH	Finish
1970	Harold's Club Transcontinental Trophy Dash		Ron Reynolds			8th, dropped out at Sioux City
1970	Reno NCAR	Qualification	Ron Reynolds		349.714	11th
1970	Reno NCAR	Heat 1	Ron Reynolds		337.190	5th
1970	Reno NCAR	Consolation	Ron Reynolds		358.524	2nd
1970	California	Qualification	Ron Reynolds			20th
1970	California	Qualification	Ron Reynolds			18th
1971	U.S. Cup Race	1000 Miles	Ron Reynolds		76 Laps	9th

Race #: 70 (1969), 77 (1970-Present)   Type: Grumman F8F-2 Bearcat   BuNo: 122619   N#: N777L

Year	Event	Heat/Race	Pilot	Aircraft's Name	Speed MPH	Finish
1969	Reno NCAR	Qualification	Lyle Shelton	*Able Cat*	357.06	6th
1969	Reno NCAR	Heat 2	Lyle Shelton	*Able Cat*	356.89	3rd
1969	Reno NCAR	Championship	Lyle Shelton	*Able Cat*	356.366	5th
1970	Reno NCAR	Qualification	Lyle Shelton	*The Able Cat*	373.460	5th
1970	Reno NCAR	Heat 1	Lyle Shelton	*The Able Cat*	369.268	1st
1970	Reno NCAR	Championship	Lyle Shelton	*The Able Cat*		7th, out 1st lap w/failed engine
1971	NAR, Cape May, New Jersey	Qualification	Lyle Shelton	*Phoenix I*	361.93	1st
1971	NAR, Cape May, New Jersey	Heat 1-A	Lyle Shelton	*Phoenix I*	305.35	2nd
1971	NAR, Cape May, New Jersey	Heat 1-B	Lyle Shelton	*Phoenix I*	350.75	2nd
1971	NAR, Cape May, New Jersey	Championship	Lyle Shelton	*Phoenix I*	360.15	1st
1971	U.S. Cup Race	1000 Miles	Lyle Shelton	*Phoenix I*	88 Laps	4th
1971	Reno NCAR	Qualification	Lyle Shelton	*Phoenix I*	418.009	2nd
1971	Reno NCAR	Qualification	Lyle Shelton	*Phoenix I*	418.009	2nd
1971	Reno NCAR	Heat 1-B	Lyle Shelton	*Phoenix I*	409.360	1st
1971	Reno NCAR	Championship	Lyle Shelton	*Phoenix I*	413.066	2nd
1972	Reno NCAR	Qualification	Lyle Shelton	*Phast Phoenix*	402.740	3rd
1972	Reno NCAR	Heat 1	Lyle Shelton	*Phast Phoenix*	389.834	2nd
1972	Reno NCAR	Championship	Lyle Shelton	*Phast Phoenix*	404.703	2nd
1973	Great Miami Air Race	Qualification	Lyle Shelton	*US Thrift*	360.795	5th
1973	Great Miami Air Race	Heat 2	Lyle Shelton	*US Thrift*	268.60	2nd
1973	Great Miami Air Race	Heat 1-A	Lyle Shelton	*US Thrift*	360.331	1st
1973	Great Miami Air Race	Turner Speed Classic	Lyle Shelton	*US Thrift*	373.320	1st
1973	Reno NCAR	Qualification	Lyle Shelton	*US Thrift*	426.602	1st, New Record
1973	Reno NCAR	Heat 1	Lyle Shelton	*US Thrift*	406.140	1st
1973	Reno NCAR	Championship	Lyle Shelton	*US Thrift*	428.155	1st, New Record
1973	California Air Races	Qualification	Lyle Shelton	*US Thrift*	341.666	7th

Year	Event	Race	Pilot	Aircraft	Speed	Result
1973	California Air Races	Heat 1-B	Lyle Shelton	US Thrift	372.492	2nd
1973	California Air Races	Championship	Lyle Shelton	US Thrift	396.614	1st
1973	California Air Races	Drag Race	Lyle Shelton	US Thrift	228.837	5th
1974	Reno NCAR	Qualification	Lyle Shelton	Omni Special	432.252	1st, New Record
1974	Reno NCAR	Heat 1	Lyle Shelton	Omni Special	420.118	1st
1974	Reno NCAR	Championship	Lyle Shelton	Omni Special	431+	1st , but later dropped to 5th for Mayday infraction.
1974	California NAR	Qualification	Lyle Shelton	Omni Special	413.737	1st
1974	California NAR	Heat	Lyle Shelton	Omni Special	312.282	3rd
1974	California NAR	Silver	Lyle Shelton	Omni Special		Did Not Finish
1974	California NAR	Championship	Lyle Shelton	Omni Special	381.719	2nd
1975	California NAR	Qualification	Lyle Shelton	Aircraft Cylinder & Turbine	406.97	2nd
1975	California NAR	Championship	Lyle Shelton	Aircraft Cylinder & Turbine	421.69	2nd
1975	Reno NAR	Qualification	Lyle Shelton	Aircraft Cylinder & Turbine	423.529	2nd
1975	Reno NAR	Medallion	Lyle Shelton	Aircraft Cylinder & Turbine		Out Lap 5
1975	Reno NAR	Championship	Lyle Shelton	Aircraft Cylinder & Turbine	429.916	1st, New Record
1975	California NAR	Qualification	Lyle Shelton	Spirit of '77'		Crashed during qualifying
1980	Reno NAR	Qualification	Lyle Shelton	Rare Bear	402.753	4th
1980	Reno NAR	Gold Heat 1	Lyle Shelton	Rare Bear		Did Not Start
1980	Reno NAR	Gold Heat 2	Lyle Shelton	Rare Bear		Did Not Start
1981	Reno NAR	Qualification	Lyle Shelton	Rare Bear	416.037	6th
1981	Reno NAR	Gold Heat 1	Lyle Shelton	Rare Bear	416.721	1st
1981	Reno NAR	Gold Heat 2	Lyle Shelton	Rare Bear		Out lap 2
1983	Reno NAR	Qualification	Lyle Shelton	Rare Bear	432.047	5th
1983	Reno NAR	Gold Heat 1	Lyle Shelton	Rare Bear	415.736	3rd
1983	Reno NAR	Gold Heat 2	Lyle Shelton	Rare Bear	432.339	3rd
1981	Reno NAR	Gold	Lyle Shelton	Rare Bear		Out lap 8
1985	Bakersfield NAR	Qualification	Lyle Shelton	Rare Bear	418.774	3rd
1985	Bakersfield NAR	Gold Heat	Lyle Shelton	Rare Bear	399.048	2nd
1985	Bakersfield NAR	Gold	Lyle Shelton	Rare Bear	408.723	2nd, cut pylon 5 on lap 3
1985	Reno NAR	Qualification	John Penny	Rare Bear	429.485	7th
1985	Reno NAR	Heat 1-A	John Penny	Rare Bear	407.502	1st, cut pylon 2 on Pace Lap
1985	Reno NAR	Gold Heat 2	John Penny	Rare Bear		Out lap 6
1986	Reno NAR	Qualification	John Penny	Rare Bear	402.171	9th
1986	Reno NAR	Heat 1-A	John Penny	Rare Bear	398.032	2nd
1986	Reno NAR	Heat 2-B	John Penny	Rare Bear	419.783	2nd
1986	Reno NAR	Heat 3-B	John Penny	Rare Bear	406.870	1st
1986	Reno NAR	Gold	John Penny	Rare Bear	407.565	5th
1987	Reno NAR	Qualification	Lyle Shelton	Rare Bear	452.490	3rd
1987	Reno NAR	Heat 2-A	Lyle Shelton	Rare Bear	396.361	5th
1987	Reno NAR	Heat 3-A	Lyle Shelton	Rare Bear	430.553	3rd
1987	Reno NAR	Gold	Lyle Shelton	Rare Bear		Out lap 2
1988	Wings of Victory Air Races	Qualification	Lyle Shelton	Rare Bear	411.095	1st
1988	Wings of Victory Air Races	Gold	Lyle Shelton	Rare Bear	412.492	1st
1988	Reno NAR	Qualification	Lyle Shelton	Rare Bear	474.622	1st, New Record
1988	Reno NAR	Heat 2-A	Lyle Shelton	Rare Bear	423.401	3rd
1988	Reno NAR	Heat 3-A	Lyle Shelton	Rare Bear		Out mid-race
1988	Reno NAR	Gold	Lyle Shelton	Rare Bear	456.821	1st, New Record
1989	Reno NAR	Qualification	Lyle Shelton	Rare Bear	467.387	1st
1989	Reno NAR	Heat 2-A	Lyle Shelton	Rare Bear	443.331	1st
1989	Reno NAR	Heat 3-A	Lyle Shelton	Rare Bear	445.805	1st
1989	Reno NAR	Gold	Lyle Shelton	Rare Bear	450.910	1st
1990	Reno NAR	Qualification	Lyle Shelton	Rare Bear	468.369	2nd
1990	Reno NAR	Heat 2-A	Lyle Shelton	Rare Bear	454.653	1st
1990	Reno NAR	Heat 3-A	Lyle Shelton	Rare Bear	452.358	1st
1990	Reno NAR	Gold	Lyle Shelton	Rare Bear	468.620	1st, New Record
1991	Reno NAR	Qualification	Lyle Shelton	Rare Bear	475.899	1st, New Record
1991	Reno NAR	Heat 2-A	John Penny	Rare Bear	452.348	2nd
1991	Reno NAR	Heat 3-A	Lyle Shelton	Rare Bear	465.385	1st
1991	Reno NAR	Gold	Lyle Shelton	Rare Bear	481.618	1st, New Record
1992	Reno NAR	Qualification	Lyle Shelton	Rare Bear	482.892	1st, New Record
1992	Reno NAR	Heat 2.A	Lyle Shelton	Rare Bear		Did Not Finish
1992	Reno NAR	Heat 3-A	Lyle Shelton	Rare Bear	449.984	2nd
1992	Reno NAR	Gold	Lyle Shelton	Rare Bear		Out lap 5
1994	Phoenix 500 Air Races	Qualification	John Penny	Rare Bear	379.674	9th
1994	Phoenix 500 Air Races	Heat 1-A	John Penny	Rare Bear	404.908	3rd, cut pylon 7 on laps 3 and 5
1994	Phoenix 500 Air Races	Gold	John Penny	Rare Bear	434.158	1st, cut pylon 6 on lap 1
1994	Reno NAR	Qualification	John Penny	Rare Bear	471.325	1st
1994	Reno NAR	Heat 2-A	John Penny	Rare Bear	462.188	1st
1994	Reno NAR	Heat 3-A	John Penny	Rare Bear	443.296	1st
1994	Reno NAR	Super Gold Shootout	John Penny	Rare Bear	424.407	1st
1995	Phoenix 500 Air Races	Qualification	John Penny	Rare Bear	470.427	1st
1995	Phoenix 500 Air Races	Pro Heat 2-A	John Penny	Rare Bear	443.372	1st
1995	Reno NAR	Qualification	John Penny	Rare Bear	489.802	1st
1995	Reno NAR	Heat 2-A	John Penny	Rare Bear	455.856	2nd
1995	Reno NAR	Heat 3-A	John Penny	Rare Bear	462.329	2nd
1995	Reno NAR	Gold	John Penny	Rare Bear	465.159	2nd
1996	Reno NAR	Qualification	John Penny	Rare Bear	491.266	1st, New Record
1996	Reno NAR	Heat 2-A	John Penny	Rare Bear	473.160	3rd
1996	Reno NAR	Gold	John Penny	Rare Bear		Out lap 2
1997	Reno NAR	Qualification	Lyle Shelton	Rare Bear	461.508	2nd
1997	Reno NAR	Heat 2-A	Lyle Shelton	Rare Bear	455.397	2nd
1997	Reno NAR	Heat 3-A	Lyle Shelton	Rare Bear	445.346	2nd
1997	Reno NAR	Gold	Lyle Shelton	Rare Bear	423.809	3rd
1999	Reno NAR	Qualification	John Penny	Rare Bear	468.780	3rd
1999	Reno NAR	Heat 2-A	Matt Jackson	Rare Bear		Did Not Finish
1999	Reno NAR	Heat 3-A	Lyle Shelton	Rare Bear	373.293	6th, 5 laps

Race #: 80 (1964), 41 (1973)   **Type:** Grumman F8F-2 Bearcat   **BuNo:** 121751   **N#:** N9885C

Year	Event	Race	Pilot	Aircraft's Name	MPH	Finish
1964	Reno NCAR	Qualification	Mira Slovak	*Smirnoff*	356.29	3rd
1964	Reno NCAR	Heat 2	Mira Slovak	*Smirnoff*	345.98	1st
1964	Reno NCAR	Heat 4	Mira Slovak	*Smirnoff*	344.04	1st
1964	Reno NCAR	Championship	Mira Slovak	*Smirnoff*	355.52	1st
1965	Los Angeles NAR	Qualification	Mira Slovak	*Smirnoff*	296.00	6th
1965	Los Angeles NAR	Heat 1	Mira Slovak	*Smirnoff*	359.72	1st
1965	Los Angeles NAR	Heat 3	Mira Slovak	*Smirnoff*	350.84	3rd
1965	Los Angeles NAR	Championship	Mira Slovak	*Smirnoff*	369.64	3rd
1965	Reno NCAR	Qualification	Mira Slovak	*Smirnoff*	338.03	4th
1965	Reno NCAR	Heat 2	Mira Slovak	*Smirnoff*	345.74	3 rd
1965	Reno NCAR	Heat 3	Mira Slovak	*Smirnoff*	345.57	3 rd
1965	Reno NCAR	Championship	Mira Slovak	*Smirnoff*	356.00	4th
1965	Las Vegas IAR	Qualification	Mira Slovak	*Smirnoff*	349.17	6th
1965	Las Vegas IAR	Heat 1-B	Mira Slovak	*Smirnoff*	359.27	2nd
1965	Las Vegas IAR	Heat 2-A	Mira Slovak	*Smirnoff*		Pylon Cut
1965	Las Vegas IAR	Championship	Mira Slovak	*Smirnoff*	322.23	3rd
1973	Reno NCAR	Qualification	Mike Smith	*Lois Jean*	352.096	13th
1973	Reno NCAR	Medallion	Mike Smith	*Lois Jean*		Disqualified
1973	California Air Races	Qualification	Mike Smith	*Lois Jean*	248.067	11th
1973	California Air Races	Heat 1-B	Mike Smith	*Lois Jean*	298.533	5th
1973	California Air Races	Silver	Mike Smith	*Lois Jean*	332.307	1st
1973	California Air Races	Drag Race	Mike Smith	*Lois Jean*	237.489	3rd

Race #: 98   **Type:** Grumman F8F-2 Bearcat   **BuNo:** 122637   **N#:** N198F

Year	Event	Race	Pilot	Aircraft's Name	MPH	Finish
1971	California 1000 Air Race	1000 miles	John Church		290.95	8th, 35 laps
1972	Reno NCAR	Qualification	John Church		350.348	9th
1972	Reno NCAR	Heat 1	John Church		329.514	6th
1972	Reno NCAR	Consolation	John Church		344.447	3rd
1972	Reno NCAR	Medallion	John Church		340.267	3rd
1978	Reno NCAR	Qualification	John Herlihy		358.67	12th
1978	Reno NCAR	Heat 2	John Herlihy		351.71	5th
1978	Reno NCAR	Consolation	John Herlihy		368.579	1st
1979	Reno NCAR	Qualification	John Herlihy	*Herlihy Bearcat*	371.345	12th
1979	Reno NCAR	Silver Heat 1	John Herlihy		352.053	4th
1979	Reno NCAR	Silver Heat 2	John Herlihy		352.932	3rd
1979	Reno NCAR	Silver	John Herlihy		359.314	3rd
1979	Reno NCAR	Gold	John Herlihy			Out lap 2

Race #: 99   **Type:** Grumman F8F-2 Bearcat   **BuNo:** 121528   **N#:** N212KA

Year	Event	Race	Pilot	Aircraft's Name	MPH	Finish
1968	Reno NCAR	Qualification	Bob Kucera			
1968	Reno NCAR	Heat 1-B	Bob Kucera		326.226	4th
1968	Reno NCAR	Consolation	Bob Kucera		331.851	1st

Race #: 204   **Type:** Grumman F8F-1   **BuNo:** 95255   **N#:** N41089

Year	Event	Race	Pilot	Aircraft's Name	MPH	Finish
1996	Reno NCAR	Qualification	David Price		360.474	14th
1996	Reno NCAR	Heat 1-B	David Price		347.063	3rd
1996	Reno NCAR	Heat 2-B	David Price			Did Not Start
1996	Reno NCAR	Bronze	David Price			Did Not Start
1997	Reno NCAR	Qualification	Alan Preston		367.175	19th
1997	Reno NCAR	Heat 1-C	Alan Preston		320.205	5th
1997	Reno NCAR	Heat 2-C	Alan Preston		325.212	6th, 5 laps
1997	Reno NCAR	Heat 3-C	Alan Preston		325.212	5th
1997	Reno NCAR	Bronze	Alan Preston		343.867	6th
1998	Reno NCAR	Qualification	Alan Preston		360.926	19th
1998	Reno NCAR	Heat 1-C	David Price		339.493	5th
1998	Reno NCAR	Heat 2-C	David Price		352.784	5th
1998	Reno NCAR	Heat 3-C	David Price		352.784	5th
1998	Reno NCAR	Bronze	Alan Preston		350.363	3rd
1999	Reno NCAR	Qualification	Alan Preston		365.900	20th
1999	Reno NCAR	Heat 1-B	David Price		325.628	4th, 5 laps
1999	Reno NCAR	Heat 2-C	Skip Holm		283.232	5th, 5 laps
1999	Reno NCAR	Heat 3-C	Skip Holm			Did Not Finish
1999	Reno NCAR	Bronze	Skip Holm		347.182	3rd

CORSAIR RACERS

RACING CORSAIRS LISTED BY RACE NUMBER

CLEVELAND ERA

Race	Pilot	Name	Reg. No.	Type	BuNo.	Notes
90	Thomas Call	*Joe*	NX63382	FG-1D	88086	
92	Cook Cleland	*Lucky Gallon*	NX66900	FG-1A	13481	
18	Ron Puckett	*Betty*	N91092	XF2G-1	14694	(also named *Miss Port Columbus*)
57	Cleland/McKillen		N5588N	F2G-2	88458	
74	Becker		N5577N	F2G-2	88463	
84	Janazzo		N5588N	F2G-1	88457	
94	Becker/Cleland		N5590N	XF2G-1	14693	

RENO ERA

Race	Pilot	Name	Reg. No.	Type	BuNo.	Notes
0	Jim Maloney	*The Chino Kids*	N83782	F4U-1	17799	
1	Hinton/Maloney/Eldridge	*Super Corsair*	N31518	F4U-1		
2	Lynn Whinney		N4719C	FG-1D	92081	(Raced once at Los Angeles NAR, crashed, Whinney killed)
5	Merle Gustafson	*Angel of Okinawa*	N5215V	F4U-4	97286	
6	Howard Pardue		N67HP	FG-1D	92095	
12	Alan Preston	*Ole Dead Eye*	N4901W	F4U-5NL	124560	
22	Gene Akers	*Lancer Two*	N6667	F4U-4	97259	
37	J.K. "Buck" Ridley	*Big Richard*	N4908M	F4U-4	96995	
82	Mike Wright	*Wart Hog*	N4715C	FG-1D	67089	
86	Ron Reynolds	*Whistling Death*	N92509	FG-1D	92509	(Raced once at Cape May, NJ, 1971)
93	Bob Guilford	*Blue Max*	NX33693	F4U-7	133693	
94	Bob Mitchem	*Big Hummer*	N194G	FG-1D	92050	
101	Bob Yancey	*Old Blue*	N49092	F4U-4	97280	
111	Gary Meermans	*Sky Boss*	N97GM	FG-1D	67089	
115	Dennis Bradley		C-GCWX	FG-1D	92436	(Raced once at Homestead, Florida)

CORSAIR D RACERS

Race #: 18   **Type:** Goodyear XF2G-1   **BuNo:** 14694   **N#:** N91092

Year	Event	Race	Pilot	Aircraft's Name	MPH	Finish
1947	Clevealnd NAR	Qualification	Ron Puckett		371.415	7th
1947	Cleveland NAR	Thompson	Ron Puckett			7th, out 19th lap
1948	Cleveland NAR	Qualification	Ron Puckett			Did Not Qualify
1949	Cleveland NAR	Qualification	Ron Puckett	*Miss Port Columbus/Betty*	373.523	11th
1949	Cleveland NAR	Sohio	Ron Puckett	*Miss Port Columbus/Betty*	384.888	2nd
1949	Cleveland NAR	Thompson	Ron Puckett	*Miss Port Columbus/Betty*	393.527	2nd

Race #: 57   **Type:** Goodyear F2G-2   **BuNo:** 88458   **N#:** N5588N

Year	Event	Race	Pilot	Aircraft's Name	MPH	Finish
1949	Cleveland NAR	Qualification	Ben McKillen		396.280	4th
1948	Cleveland NAR	Tinnerman	Ben McKillen		386.069	1st
1949	Cleveland NAR	Thompson	Ben McKillen		387.589	3rd

Race #: 74   **Type:** Goodyear F2G-2   **BuNo:** 88463   **N#:** N5577N

Year	Event	Race	Pilot	Aircraft's Name	MPH	Finish
1947	Cleveland NAR	Qualification	Cook Cleland		401.787	1st New Record
1947	Cleveland NAR	Thompson	Cook Cleland		396.131	1st
1948	Cleveland NAR	Qualification	Dick Becker		405.882	3rd
1948	Cleveland NAR	Thompson	Dick Becker			10th , out lap 3
1949	Cleveland NAR	Qualification	Dick Becker		414.592	1st
1949	Cleveland NAR	Thompson	Dick Becker			Did Not Start

Race #: 84   **Type:** Goodyear F2G-1   **BuNo:** 88457   **N#:** N5588N

Year	Event	Race	Pilot	Aircraft's Name	MPH	Finish
1947	Cleveland NAR	Qualification	Tony Janazzo		372.417	6th
1947	Cleveland NAR	Thompson	Tony Janazzo			Crashed fatally in 7th lap

Race #: 90 (1946), 99 (1947)   **Type:** Goodyear FG-1D   **BuNo:** 88086   **N#:** NX63382

Year	Event	Race	Pilot	Aircraft's Name	MPH	Finish
1946	Cleveland NAR	Bendix	Thomas Call	*Joe*	325.612	15th
1946	Cleveland NAR	Bendix	Frank Whitton	*Joe*	320.025	7th

Race #: 92   **Type:** Goodyear FG-1A   **BuNo:** 13481   **N#:** NX66900

Year	Event	Race	Pilot	Aircraft's Name	MPH	Finish
1946	Clevealnd NAR	Qualification	Cook Cleland		361.809	6th
1946	Cleveland NAR	Thompson	Cook Cleland		357.465	6th

Race #: 94   **Type:** Goodyear X F2G-1   **BuNo:** 14693   **N#:** N5590N

Year	Event	Race	Pilot	Aircraft's Name	MPH	Finish
1947	Cleveland NAR	Qualification	Dick Becker		400.941	2nd
1947	Cleveland NAR	Thompson	Dick Becker		390.133	2nd
1948	Cleveland NAR	Qualification	Cook Cleland		417.424	2nd
1948	Cleveland NAR	Thompson	Cook Cleland			9th, Out lap 4
1949	Cleveland NAR	Qualification	Cook Cleland		407.211	2nd
1949	Cleveland NAR	Thompson	Cook Cleland		397.071	1st

Race #: 0 (1978)   **Type:** Vought F4U-1   **BuNo:** 17799   **N#:** NX83782

Year	Event	Race	Pilot	Aircraft's Name	MPH	Finish
1978	Reno NCAR	Qualification	Jim Maloney	*The Chino Kids*	314.968	21st
1978	Reno NCAR	1st Medallion	Jim Maloney	*The Chino Kids*	282.21	6th
1978	Reno NCAR	2nd Medallion	John Muszala	*The Chino Kids*	291.94	5th
1979	Reno NCAR	Qualification	Jim Maloney	*The Chino Kids*	319.638	25th

| | Race #: | 1 | | Type: | F2G Corsair | BuNo: | | N#: NX31518 | |

Year	Event	Race	Pilot	Aircraft's Name	MPH	Finish
1982	Reno NCAR	Qualification	Steve Hinton	*Bud Light Special*	413.208	4th
1982	Reno NCAR	Gold Heat 1	Steve Hinton	*Bud Light Special*	338.558	6th
1982	Reno NCAR	Silver Heat 2	Steve Hinton	*Bud Light Special*	352.524	5th
1982	Reno NCAR	Gold Heat 2	Jim Maloney	*Bud Light Special*	382.880	3rd
1982	Reno NCAR	Gold	Steve Hinton	*Bud Light Special*	362.496	4th
1983	Reno NCAR	Qualification	Steve Hinton	*Bud Light Special*	408.331	8th
1983	Reno NCAR	Silver Heat 1	Steve Hinton	*Bud Light Special*	374.619	3rd
1983	Reno NCAR	Silver Heat 2	Steve Hinton	*Bud Light Special*	403.578	1st
1983	Reno NCAR	Silver	Steve Hinton	*Bud Light Special*	417.097	1st
1984	Reno NCAR	Qualification	Steve Hinton	*Super Corsair*	424.015	8th
1984	Reno NCAR	Heat 3	Steve Hinton	*Super Corsair*	417.327	1st
1984	Reno NCAR	Heat 6	Steve Hinton	*Super Corsair*	408.631	4th
1984	Reno NCAR	Heat 9	Steve Hinton	*Super Corsair*	422.652	2nd
1984	Reno NCAR	Gold	Steve Hinton	*Super Corsair*	413.686	3rd
1985	Bakersfield NAR	Qualification	Steve Hinton	*Super Corsair*	412.999	4th
1985	Bakersfield NAR	Gold Heat	Steve Hinton	*Super Corsair*	394.408	3rd
1985	Bakersfield NAR	Gold	Steve Hinton	*Super Corsair*	394.925	3rd, cut pylon 5 on lap 3
1985	Reno NAR	Qualification	Steve Hinton	*Super Corsair*	431.944	5th
1985	Reno NAR	Heat 2-A	Steve Hinton	*Super Corsair*	421.007	2nd
1985	Reno NAR	Heat 3-A	Steve Hinton	*Super Corsair*	433.844	2nd
1985	Reno NAR	Gold	Steve Hinton	*Super Corsair*	438.186	1st
1986	Reno NAR	Qualification	John Maloney	*Super Corsair*	422.006	8th
1986	Reno NAR	Heat 1-A	John Maloney	*Super Corsair*		Did Not Finish
1986	Reno NAR	Heat 2-B	John Maloney	*Super Corsair*	314.637	6th, 5 laps
1987	Reno NAR	Qualification	John Maloney	*Super Corsair*	431.607	6th
1987	Reno NAR	Heat 2-A	John Maloney	*Super Corsair*	399.565	4th
1987	Reno NAR	Heat 3-A	John Maloney	*Super Corsair*	419.800	4th
1987	Reno NAR	Gold	John Maloney	*Super Corsair*	416.905	4th
1988	Wings of Victory Air Races	Qualification	John Maloney	*Super Corsair*	346.210	10th
1988	Wings of Victory Air Races	Silver	John Maloney	*Super Corsair*	352.630	1st
1988	Reno NAR	Qualification	John Maloney	*Super Corsair*	442.319	7th
1988	Reno NAR	Heat 1-A	John Maloney	*Super Corsair*	445.072	1st
1988	Reno NAR	Heat 2-A	John Maloney	*Super Corsair*	420.177	4th
1988	Reno NAR	Heat 3-A	John Maloney	*Super Corsair*		Out mid-race
1988	Reno NAR	Gold	John Maloney	*Super Corsair*	368.126	6th, 7 laps
1989	Reno NAR	Qualification	John Maloney	*Super Corsair*	437.583	4th
1989	Reno NAR	Heat 2-A	John Maloney	*Super Corsair*	402.090	3rd
1989	Reno NAR	Heat 3-A	John Maloney	*Super Corsair*	416.250	5th
1989	Reno NAR	Gold	John Maloney	*Super Corsair*	406.265	3rd
1990	Texas Air Races	Qualification	John Maloney	*Super Corsair*	381.805	4th
1990	Texas Air Races	Gold Heat	John Maloney	*Super Corsair*	356.101	4th
1990	Texas Air Races	Gold	John Maloney	*Super Corsair*	376.479	4th
1990	Colorado NAR	Qualification	John Maloney	*Super Corsair*	421.671	2nd
1990	Colorado NAR	Gold Heat	John Maloney	*Super Corsair*		Out lap 5
1990	Colorado NAR	Gold	John Maloney	*Super Corsair*	389.332	3rd
1990	Reno NAR	Qualification	John Maloney	*Super Corsair*	426.653	5th
1990	Reno NAR	Heat 2-A	John Maloney	*Super Corsair*	406.945	6th
1990	Reno NAR	Heat 3-A	John Maloney	*Super Corsair*	415.224	5th
1990	Reno NAR	Gold	John Maloney	*Super Corsair*	410.786	5th
1991	Reno NAR	Qualification	John Maloney	*Super Corsair*	434.207	6th
1991	Reno NAR	Heat 2-A	John Maloney	*Super Corsair*	377.832	7th, 5 laps
1991	Reno NAR	Heat 3-A	John Maloney	*Super Corsair*	410.179	6th
1991	Reno NAR	Gold	John Maloney	*Super Corsair*	406.420	7th, 7 laps
1992	Reno NAR	Qualification	John Maloney	*Super Corsair*	425.603	7th
1992	Reno NAR	Heat 1-A	Kevin Eldridge	*Super Corsair*	429.937	2nd
1992	Reno NAR	Heat 2-B	Kevin Eldridge	*Super Corsair*	423.164	1st
1992	Reno NAR	Heat 3-A	Kevin Eldridge	*Super Corsair*	411.291	7th
1992	Reno NAR	Gold	Kevin Eldridge	*Super Corsair*	420.800	6th
1993	Reno NAR	Qualification	John Maloney	*Super Corsair*	426.155	6th
1993	Reno NAR	Heat 2-A	Kevin Eldridge	*Super Corsair*		Out lap 4
1993	Reno NAR	Heat 3-A	Kevin Eldridge	*Super Corsair*	377.522	5th
1993	Reno NAR	Gold	Kevin Eldridge	*Super Corsair*	418.656	5th
1993	Kansas City Air Races	Qualification	Kevin Eldridge	*Super Corsair*	377.73	5th
1993	Kansas City Air Races	Heat 3	Kevin Eldridge	*Super Corsair*	362.24	1st, cut pylon 3 on pace lap
1993	Kansas City Air Races	Championship	Kevin Eldridge	*Super Corsair*	375.84	4th
1994	Phoenix 500 Air Races	Qualification	Kevin Eldridge	*Super Corsair*	428.104	4th
1994	Phoenix 500 Air Races	Heat 1-A	Kevin Eldridge	*Super Corsair*	355.440	6th
1994	Phoenix 500 Air Races	Heat 2-B	Kevin Eldridge	*Super Corsair*		Out lap 3, crashed after fire

| Race #: | 2 | Type: | | Goodyear FG-1D | BuNo: 92081 | N#: N4719C |

Year	Event	Race	Pilot	Aircraft's Name	MPH	Finish
1966	Los Angeles NAR	Qualification	Lynn Winney		———	Didn't Qualify (Lynn Winney was killed in a crash while practicing)

| Race #: | 3 (1970), 93 (1971) | Type: | Vought F4U-7 | BuNo: 133693 | N#: N693M |

Year	Event	Race	Pilot	Aircraft's Name	Speed MPH	Finish
1970	California 1000	Qualification	Bob Guilford		280.42	16th
1970	California 1000	Race	Bob Guilford			16th, 47 Laps
1971	Alton P-51 Tournament	30 Second Climb Out	Bob Guilford	*Blue Max*	670 ft.	9th

Year	Event	Heat/Race	Pilot	Aircraft's Name	MPH	Finish
1971	Alton P-51 Tournament	1 Mile Course	Bob Guilford	*Blue Max*	352.9	4th
1971	U.S. Cup Race	1000 Miles	Bob Guilford	*Blue Max*	72 Laps	10th
1971	Reno NCAR	Qualification	Bob Guilford	*Blue Max*	289.655	16th
1971	Reno NCAR	Medallion	Bob Guilford	*Blue Max*	264.766	2nd
1971	California 100 Mile Race	1000 Miles	Bob Guilford	*Blue Max*	264.16	10th, 32 laps
1973	Reno NCAR	Qualification	Bob Guilford	*Blue Max*		Did Not Qualify
1974	Reno NCAR	Qualification	Bob Guilford	*Blue Max*	304.615	17th
1974	Reno NCAR	Consolation	Bob Guilford	*Blue Max*	267.262	5th
1974	Reno NCAR	Medallion	Bob Guilford	*Blue Max*	283.232	Disqualified
1974	California NAR	Qualification	Bob Guilford	*Blue Max*	296.684	11th
1974	California NAR	Heat	Bob Guilford	*Blue Max*	258.621	7th
1974	California NAR	Silver	Bob Guilford	*Blue Max*	261.544	7th
1974	California NAR	Championship	Bob Guilford	*Blue Max*		9th, cut pylon 5 on lap 1
1975	California NAR	Qualification	Bob Guilford	*Blue Max*	305.08	16th
1975	California NAR	Silver	Bob Guilford	*Blue Max*	260.90	9th
1975	Reno NCAR	Qualification	Bob Guilford	*Blue Max*	307.050	20th
1975	Reno NCAR	Medallion	Bob Guilford	*Blue Max*	241.534	6th
1979	California NAR	Qualification	Bob Guilford	*Blue Max*	281.302	9th
1979	California NAR	Silver Speed Sprint	Bob Guilford	*Blue Max*	260.559	4th
1979	California NAR	Drag Race	Bob Guilford	*Blue Max*	225.414	5th
1979	California NAR	Unlimited Gold Sprint	Bob Guilford	*Blue Max*	249.279	5th
1979	Reno NCAR	Qualification	Bob Guilford	*Blue Max*	330.702	22nd
1979	Reno NCAR	Bronze Heat 1	Bob Guilford	*Blue Max*	258.264	6th
1979	Reno NCAR	Bronze Heat 2	Bob Guilford	*Blue Max*		Out last lap
1980	Reno NCAR	Qualification	Bob Guilford	*Blue Max*	312.950	21st
1980	Reno NCAR	Bronze Heat 1	Bob Guilford	*Blue Max*	285.109	6th
1980	Reno NCAR	Bronze Heat 2	Bob Guilford	*Blue Max*	249.333	7th
1980	Reno NCAR	Bronze	Bob Guilford	*Blue Max*	239.598	6th
1981	Reno NCAR	Qualification	Bob Guilford	*Blue Max*	324.665	22nd
1981	Reno NCAR	Bronze	Bob Guilford	*Blue Max*	247.779	4th
1982	Reno NCAR	Qualification	Bob Guilford	*Blue Max*	333.433	20th
1982	Reno NCAR	Bronze Heat 1	Bob Guilford	*Blue Max*	265.698	6th
1982	Reno NCAR	Bronze Heat 2	Bob Guilford	*Blue Max*	297.078	5th
1982	Reno NCAR	Bronze	Bob Guilford	*Blue Max*	308.375	4th
1983	Reno NCAR	Qualification	Bob Guilford	*Blue Max*	316.671	27th
1983	Reno NCAR	Medallion 1	Bob Guilford	*Blue Max*		Did Not Start
1983	Reno NCAR	Medallion 2	Bob Guilford	*Blue Max*	247.467	5th
1985	Reno NCAR	Qualification	Bob Guilford	*Blue Max*	326.732	28th
1985	Reno NCAR	Bronze	Bob Guilford	*Blue Max*	282.904	9th
1986	Reno NCAR	Qualification	Bob Guilford	*Blue Max*	325.994	29th
1986	Reno NCAR	Bronze	Bob Guilford	*Blue Max*	264.586	8th, 5 laps

Race #: 12 *Type:* Vought F4U-5NL *BuNo:* 124560 *N#:* N4901W

Year	Event	Heat/Race	Pilot	Aircraft's Name	MPH	Finish
1985	Reno NCAR	Qualification	Alan Preston	*Old Deadeye*	332.891	27th
1985	Reno NCAR	Heat 1-C	Alan Preston	*Old Deadeye*		Did Not Finish
1985	Reno NCAR	Bronze	Alan Preston	*Old Deadeye*	314.878	6 th

Race #: 22 *Type:* Vought F4U-4 *BuNo:* 97259 *N#:* N6667

Year	Event	Heat/Race	Pilot	Aircraft's Name	MPH	Finish
1967	Reno NCAR	Qualification	Gene Akers		316.37	10th
1967	Reno NCAR	Consolation	Gene Akers		300.78	4th
1968	Reno NCAR	Qualification	Gene Akers			
1968	Reno NCAR	Heat 1-B	Gene Akers	*Lancer Two*		Did Not Start
1968	Reno NCAR	Consolation	Gene Akers	*Lancer Two*	301.537	3rd
1969	Harold's Club Transcontinental Trophy Dash		Dick Thomas		217.860	9th, finished after deadline
1969	Reno NCAR	Qualification	Gene Akers	*Lancer Two*	281.25	13th
1969	Reno NCAR	Heat 2	Gene Akers	*Lancer Two*	296.11	6th
1970	California 1000	Qualification	Gene Akers	*Lancer Two*	282.82	15th
1970	California 1000	Race	Gene Akers	*Lancer Two*		14th, 55 Laps
1971	U.S. Cup Race	1000 Miles	Gene Akers			6th, 84 Laps
1971	California 1000 Air Race	1000 Miles	Carl Birdwell		314.97	5th, 38 laps

Race #: 37 *Type:* Vought F4U-4 *BuNo:* 96995 *N#:* N4908M

Year	Event	Heat/Race	Pilot	Aircraft's Name	MPH	Finish
1984	Reno NCAR	Qualification	J.K. Ridley		316.248	26th
1984	Reno NCAR	Heat 1	J.K. Ridley			Out lap 5
1984	Reno NCAR	Heat 7	J.K. Ridley		291.132	Cut pylon 3 on lap 6
1984	Reno NCAR	Bronze	J.K. Ridley		320.922	4th
1985	Reno NCAR	Qualification	J.K. Ridley	*Big Richard*	338.767	26th
1985	Reno NCAR	Heat 1-C	J.K. Ridley	*Big Richard*	321.703	4th
1985	Reno NCAR	Heat 3-C	J.K. Ridley	*Big Richard*		Did Not Start
1985	Reno NCAR	Bronze	J.K. Ridley	*Big Richard*	324.575	5th

Race #: 67 (1979)   **Type:** *Goodyear FG-1D*   **BuNo:** *92095*   **N#:** *N67HP*

Year	Event	Race	Pilot	Aircraft's Name	MPH	Finish
1979	Miami, International AR	Qualification	Howard Pardue		241.610	27th
1979	Miami, International AR	Stock Heat 1	Howard Pardue		221.149	5th
1979	Miami, International AR	Stock Heat 1	Howard Pardue		242.167	7th
1979	Miami, International AR	Final Stock Race	Howard Pardue		250.447	7th

Race #: 82   **Type:** *Goodyear FG-1D*   **BuNo:** *67089*   **N#:** *N4715C*

Year	Event	Race	Pilot	Aircraft's Name	MPH	Finish
1982	Reno NCAR	Qualification	Mike Wright	*Wart Hog*	304.038	22nd
1982	Reno NCAR	Bronze	Mike Wright	*Wart Hog*	275.610	5th
1984	Canadian IAR	Qualification	Mike Wright	*Wart Hog*	299.660	12th
1984	Canadian IAR	Silver Practice	Mike Wright	*Wart Hog*		Out lap 8
1984	Canadian IAR	Petro-Canada Cup	Mike Wright	*Wart Hog*		Did Not Start
1984	Reno NCAR	Qualification	Mike Wright	*Wart Hog*	305.667	28th
1984	Reno NCAR	Heat 1	Mike Wright	*Wart Hog*	275.388	3rd
1984	Reno NCAR	Heat 7	Mike Wright	*Wart Hog*	203.229	8th, 4 laps
1984	Reno NCAR	Bronze	Mike Wright	*Wart Hog*	285.065	5th, out lap 6

Race #: 86 (1971)   **Type:** *Goodyear FG-1D*   **BuNo:** *92905*   **N#:** *N92509*

Year	Event	Heat/Race	Pilot	Aircraft's Name	MPH	Finish
1971	NAR, Cape May, New Jersy	Qualification	Ron Reynolds	*Whistling Death*	310.71	5th

Race #: 94 (1967) Type: *Goodyear FG-1D*   **BuNo:** *92050*   **N#:** *N194G*

Year	Event	Heat/Race	Pilot	Aircraft's Name	MPH	Finish
1967	Reno NCAR	Qualification	Bob Mitchem	*Big Hummer*		Did Not Qualify
1970	Reno NCAR	Qualification	Bob Mitchem	*Big Hummer*	362.989	7th
1970	Reno NCAR	Heat 1	Bob Mitchem	*Big Hummer*	344.401	4th
1970	Reno NCAR	Consolation	Bob Mitchem	*Big Hummer*	357.947	3rd
1971	Reno NCAR	Qualification	Bob Mitchem	*Big Hummer*	342.192	17th
1972	Reno NCAR	Qualification	Bob Mitchem	*Big Hummer*	367.500	7th
1972	Reno NCAR	Heat 1	Bob Mitchem	*Big Hummer*	363.087	4th

Race #: 101   **Type:** *Vought F4U-4*   **BuNo:** *97280*   **N#:** *N49092*

Year	Event	Race	Pilot	Aircraft's Name	MPH	Finish
1981	Reno NCAR	Qualification	Bob Yancey		334.933	19th
1981	Reno NCAR	Bronze Heat 1	Bob Yancey		315.635	6 th
1981	Reno NCAR	Bronze Heat 2	Bob Yancey		327.652	6 th
1981	Reno NCAR	Bronze	Bob Yancey		325.765	3rd
1982	Reno NCAR	Qualification	Bob Yancey	*Old Blue*	346.861	17th
1982	Reno NCAR	Bronze Heat 1	Bob Yancey	*Old Blue*	341.348	2nd
1982	Reno NCAR	Bronze Heat 2	Bob Yancey	*Old Blue*	341.377	2nd
1982	Reno NCAR	Bronze	Bob Yancey	*Old Blue*	355.530	2nd
1983	Reno NCAR	Qualification	Bob Yancey	*Old Blue*	370.817	15th
1983	Reno NCAR	Bronze Heat 1	Bob Yancey	*Old Blue*	362.592	2nd
1983	Reno NCAR	Silver Heat 2	Bob Yancey	*Old Blue*	332.060	5th
1983	Reno NCAR	Bronze	Bob Yancey	*Old Blue*	362.651	3rd
1984	Canadian IAR	Qualification	Bob Yancey	*Old Blue*	351.881	8th
1984	Canadian IAR	Silver Practice	Bob Yancey	*Old Blue*	306.834	1st
1984	Canadian IAR	Petro-Canada Cup	Bob Yancey	*Old Blue*	324.416	3rd
1984	Reno NCAR	Qualification	Bob Yancey	*Old Blue*	341.313	21st
1984	Reno NCAR	Heat 1	Bob Yancey	*Old Blue*	349.033	1 st
1984	Reno NCAR	Heat 4	Bob Yancey	*Old Blue*	374.216	1 st
1984	Reno NCAR	Heat 8	Bob Yancey	*Old Blue*	363.495	4 th
1985	Reno NCAR	Qualification	Bob Yancey	*Old Blue*	386.062	19th
1985	Reno NCAR	Heat 1-B	Bob Yancey	*Old Blue*	368.819	1st
1985	Reno NCAR	Heat 2-B	Bob Yancey	*Old Blue*	365.999	4th
1985	Reno NCAR	Heat 3-B	Bob Yancey	*Old Blue*	369.825	3rd
1985	Reno NCAR	Silver	Bob Yancey	*Old Blue*	374.392	2nd
1986	Reno NCAR	Qualification	Bob Yancey	*Old Blue*	391.085	13th
1986	Reno NCAR	Heat 1-A	Bob Yancey	*Old Blue*	354.081	5th
1986	Reno NCAR	Heat 2-B	Bob Yancey	*Old Blue*	352.321	5th
1986	Reno NCAR	Heat 3-B	Bob Yancey	*Old Blue*		Did Not Finish
1986	Reno NCAR	Silver	Bob Yancey	*Old Blue*	379.772	5th

Race #: 115   **Type:** *Goodyear FG-1D Corsair*   **BuNo:** *92463*   **N#:** *C-GCWX*

Year	Event	Race	Pilot	Aircraft's Name	MPH	Finish
1979	Miami, International AR	Qualification	Dennis Bradley	*Canadian Corsair*	265.822	23rd
1979	Miami, International AR	Stock Heat 1	Dennis Bradley	*Canadian Corsair*	244.470	6th, cut pylon 3 on lap 4
1979	Miami, International AR	Stock Heat 1	Dennis Bradley	*Canadian Corsair*	268.484	6th, cut pylon
1979	Miami, International AR	Final Stcok Race	Dennis Bradley	*Canadian Corsair*	278.822	6th

FURTHER READING ON ROUND-ENGINE RACERS

Berliner, Don. *Unlimited Air Racers: The Complete History of Unlimited Class Air Racing, 1946 Thompson Trophy to 1991 Reno Gold*. Motorbooks International. Osceola, WI. 1992.

Carter, Dustin W. and Birch J. Matthews. *Mustang: The Racing Thoroughbred*. Schiffer Military History. West Chester, PA. 1992.

Chapman, John and Geoff Goodall. *Warbirds Directory: An International Survey of the World's Piston and Jet Warbird Population* (Third Edition). Warbirds Worldwide Ltd. Mansfield, Notts. England.

Grantham, A. Kevin. *P-Screamers: The History of the Surviving Lockheed P-38 Lightnings*. Pictorial Histories Publishing. Missoula, MO. 1993.

_____. "Air Racing Historians Gather In Cleveland." *In Flight Aviation News*. July 1992.

_____. *Racing P-38s*. Presentation to the Society of Air Racing Historians. 1993.

_____, and Tim Weinschenker. *1946 Cleveland National Air Races*. Presentation to Society of Air Racing Historians. 1994.

_____, and Tim Weinschenker. *1947 Cleveland National Air Races*. Presentation to Society of Air Racing Historians. 1995.

_____, and Tim Weinschenker. *1948 Cleveland National Air Races*. Presentation to Society of Air Racing Historians. 1996.

_____, and Tim Weinschenker. *1949 Cleveland National Air Races*. Presentation to Society of Air Racing Historians. 1997.

_____, and Jackie Grantham. *Unlimiteds Thunder At Reno '97*. Avweb. http://www.avweb.com/articles/reno97.html

_____, and Jackie Grantham. *Reno Unlimiteds Turn 35*. Avweb. http://www.avweb.com/articles/reno98.html

_____, and Jackie Grantham. "Reno Report '97" *Warbirds Worldwide*. Issue 43.

_____, and Jackie Grantham. "Reno '98" *Warbirds Worldwide*. Issue 47.

_____, and Jackie Grantham. "Reno '99" *Warbirds Worldwide*. Issue 51.

_____, and Jackie Grantham. "Levitz-Rogers Racer," *Warbirds Worldwide*. Issue 38.

_____, and Jackie Grantham. "Miss Ashley II Update," *Warbirds Worldwide*. Issue 43.

_____, and Nicholas A. Veronico. *Raceplanes Tech Series, Vol. One: Racing Griffon-Powered Mustangs*. Specialty Press. North Branch, MN. 2000.

Kinert, Reed. *Racing Planes and Air Races*. Various editions. Aero Publishers. Fallbrook, CA. 1972,

Larsen, Jim. *Directory of Unlimited Class Pylon Air Racers*. American Air Museum. Kirkland, Washington. 1971.

_____. "Year of the Red Baron," *Air Classics*. Feb.1978.

Matthews, Birch. *Wet Wings and Drop Tanks: Recollections of American Transcontinental Air Racing, 1928–1970*. Schiffer Aviation History. Atglen, PA. 1993.

O'Leary, Michael. "Races, Records, and Disaster." *Air Classics*. Feb. 1974.

Tegler, John. *"Gentlemen, You Have A Race:" A History of the Reno National Championship Air Races 1964–1983*. Wings Publishing. Severna Park, MD. 1984.

_____. "Who's On First?" *Air Classics*. Feb. 1975.

_____. "Unlimiteds At Mojave." *Air Classics*. Oct. 1975.

_____. "Heavy Metal At Reno." *Air Classics*. Jan. 1976.

_____. "Mustangs Over Mojave." *Air Classics*. Nov. 1976.

_____. "Bang! The Unlimiteds at the 1976 Reno National Air Races." *Air Classics*. Jan. 1977.

_____. "Unlimiteds Over Reno." *Air Classics*. Jan. 1979.

_____. "The R.B. Reigns Supreme." *Air Classics*. Mar. 1979.

_____. "Racers Over Mojave." *Air Classics*. Oct. 1979.

_____. "Phoenix Rising?" *Air Classics*. Aug. 1995.

Veronico, Nicholas A. *F4U Corsair: The Combat, Development, and Racing History of the Corsair*. Motorbooks International. Osceola, WI. 1994.

_____. "Whittington Walks Away From 'Precious Metal.'" *In Flight Aviation News*. Oct. 1988.

_____. "Lyle Shelton Wins Unlimited Gold At Reno Races '88." *In Flight Aviation News*. Oct. 1988.

_____. "Rare Bear Does It Again, Wins Reno Gold." *In Flight Aviation News*. Oct. 1989.

_____. "Shelton, Rare Bear Win Third Gold." *In Flight Aviation News*. Oct. 1990.

_____. "Shelton Wins Reno: Fourth Year In A Row." *In Flight Aviation News*. Oc. 1991.

_____. "Strega Wins Unlimited Gold At 29th Reno Races." *In Flight Aviation News*. Oct. 1992.

_____. "Gentlemen—you have a race! Action From Reno." *FlyPast* magazine. Dec. 1992.

_____. "Fire Breather! Action From The 30th Reno Races." *FlyPast* magazine. Dec. 1993.

_____, A. Kevin Grantham, and Scott Thompson. *Military Aircraft Boneyards*. MBI Publishing Co., Osceola, WI. 2000.